AF735514

Corporate Acquisitions and Mergers in Finland

Corporate Acquisitions and Mergers in Finland

Timo Airistot

White & Case

This book was originally published as a chapter in Corporate Acquisitions and Mergers.

General Editor: Peter Begg

Wolters Kluwer

Published by:
Kluwer Law International B.V.
PO Box 316
2400 AH Alphen aan den Rijn
The Netherlands
E-mail: lrs-sales@wolterskluwer.com
Website: www.wolterskluwer.com/en/solutions/kluwerlawinternational

Sold and distributed by:
Wolters Kluwer Legal & Regulatory U.S.
7201 McKinney Circle
Frederick, MD 21704
United States of America
E-mail: customer.service@wolterskluwer.com

ISBN 978-94-035-2406-1

e-Book: ISBN 978-94-035-2756-7
web-PDF: ISBN 978-94-035-2766-6

Contents

White & Case

The Helsinki office of White & Case has a leading mergers and acquisitions law practice in Finland. The Helsinki office of White & Case advises multi-national corporates, private equity and venture capital firms and others on domestic and cross-border mergers, acquisitions and divestitures, controlled auctions, public tender offers, leveraged buy-outs, joint ventures and privatizations across the full range of industry sectors. The Helsinki office of White & Case typically advises Finnish clients on the full range of mergers and acquisitions activities within Finland and around the world and non-Finnish clients in their Finnish and regional activities.

For further information on the Helsinki office of White & Case, please contact:

Timo Airisto

White & Case

Aleksanterinkatu 44

FI-00100 Helsinki

Finland

Tel.: + 358 9 228 641

Fax: + 358 9 228 64 228

Author

Timo Airisto is a partner in White & Case Global M&A team. He advises international and local clients in corporate transactions. Timo has advised on some of Finland's largest transactions for the past two decades and his record of accomplishment includes private transactions, as well as public tender offers and mergers.

Timo is dual qualified in US and Finland and is also well-known for his skills in the field of cross-border real estate deals. He has advised a number of leading investors, guiding them through major real estate transactions in Finland.

1 LOCAL ECONOMIC, POLITICAL AND CULTURAL ASPECTS

1.1 Population, Language, Currency

[01] Finland is located in Northern Europe and shares borders with Sweden, Norway and Russia. As one of the Nordic countries, the country shares a common cultural and historical heritage with Denmark, Sweden, Norway and Iceland. With respect to their legal systems, the Nordic countries have cooperated in the development of unified legislation in several fields. Finland shares with Russia a 1 300 km border, which is the longest eastern border of the European Union (the EU).

[02] The country has a population of approximately 5.5 million with a population density of approximately 18 inhabitants per km^2. In 2020, 86.5% of the population lived in urban areas. Helsinki is the capital and the largest city, which has a population of approximately 650 000. The annual population growth in Finland is approximately 0.3–0.5%, which is mostly fuelled by immigration. The cities of Helsinki, Espoo, Vantaa and Kauniainen comprise the Helsinki Metropolitan Area where approximately one-fourth of the country's population currently resides. The other largest cities include Tampere, Turku and Oulu.

[03] The two national languages are Finnish and Swedish. People are entitled to use either language when dealing with government authorities or bilingual local authorities. In 2021, approximately 86.5% of the population comprised of native Finnish speakers while 5.2% were native Swedish speakers. There are also other smaller language minorities, such as Sami speakers and Russian speakers.

[04] Finland has abundant natural resources, the most important of which has historically been its forests. As a consequence, the country has developed an extensive forest industry and a number of related industries, such as industrial manufacturing. Due to these reasons, Finland has been home to many large corporations that manufacture machinery for the forestry and paper industries. Over the years, services and technology industries have also become significant industry sectors in Finland. Finland is also rich in minerals and metals and has a sizable mining industry.

[05] Finland enjoys good infrastructure in terms of both physical transportation and telecommunications. The country is very accessible to passengers and cargo through its many ports, airports and rail links, as well as by road from Sweden, Norway and Russia. The shortest flight path from Europe to China and Japan passes through Finland, giving the country a strategic advantage when it comes to travelling between Europe and Asia. Despite its northern location, ports and airports operate throughout the year and rarely close due to weather conditions. Travelling inside the country is generally easy and, due to extensive road traffic safety measures advocated by the government, also very safe.

[06] Finland is a member of the Economic and Monetary Union (EMU) and has the euro (EUR) as its currency, having been among the first eleven countries to join the euro area in 1999.

1.2 Government and Political System

[07] The Republic of Finland is a parliamentary democracy. Finland declared independence on 6 December 1917. Prior to that, Finland was a grand duchy in the Russian Empire and, prior to 1809, a part of the Kingdom of Sweden.

[08] The Finnish Parliament consists of 200 members in one chamber, who are elected every four years by direct vote. The latest parliamentary elections took place in 2019. Currently, Finland has a multiparty coalition cabinet which is headed by Prime Minister. The Head of State is the President of the Republic who is elected every six years for a maximum of two terms.

[09] Finland has been a Member State of the United Nations since 1955 and of the EU as well as the World Trade Organization since 1995. The European Parliament currently has fourteen Finnish MEPs, whose term of office is five years. Furthermore, Finland applied for NATO membership in May 2022.

[10] Through its membership and participation in trade alliances and associations as well as other international bodies both within the EU and worldwide, Finland is well integrated into the global financial system. Foreign investors do not face any major legislative restrictions when investing in Finnish companies (save for possible merger control and foreign direct investment approvals) and, in general, the country is not protectionist against foreign investors.

[11] Finland consistently ranks among the most politically stable countries in the world and thus offers a secure operational environment for both domestic and foreign businesses. Finland is also considered to be among the least corrupt countries in the world, according to surveys.

1.3 Overview of Legal System

[12] The Finnish legal system is a civil law system. The legislation enacted by the Finnish Parliament forms, as a rule, the basis for all legal decisions in Finland. The hierarchy of national legislation is as follows:

(i) The Constitution (731/1999, as amended).
(ii) Acts of Parliament.
(iii) Decrees issued by the President of the Republic, the Council of State and various Ministries.
(iv) Legal rules issued by lower-ranking authorities.

[13] As a civil law country, written law is generally more important than case law; however, case law may have importance when resolving questions that are not expressly addressed by written law.

[14] Legislation is enacted by the Finnish Parliament. The Council of State, the President and the Ministries may issue decrees pursuant to a law that has been enacted by the Parliament. Most bills are submitted to the Parliament as proposals of the Council of State. Before the proposal is submitted, the bill is drafted by the relevant Ministry with responsibility for the subject matter in question. The Parliament either passes, rejects or amends the bill. Ordinary laws are passed if they are backed by a majority of MPs. Amendments to the Constitution require a two-thirds majority of votes in the Parliament. Current, up-to-date legislation in Finnish and Swedish is available online at the Finlex databank of the Ministry of Justice at www.finlex.fi. The service is free of charge.

[15] In addition to written law, preparatory texts relating to national legislation are considered a source of law, including, in particular, the proposals of the Council of State and other texts produced in the Finnish Parliament and its various legislative committees. Preparatory legislative works provide information on the legislator's intent and, for that reason, such documents are used in the interpretation of legislation. Of the various court decisions, the most important sources of law are those of the highest courts, namely the Supreme Court and the Supreme Administrative Court.

[16] International treaties and other international obligations to which Finland is a signatory are also binding sources of law in Finland. The practices and procedures of the international bodies that apply such treaties also have significance as a source of law. Finland is a party to all major United Nations and Council of Europe conventions.

[17] As a Member State of the EU since 1 January 1995, Finland is also bound by the regulations and directives of the EU. EU regulations are directly applicable in all Member States whereas EU directives must be implemented by the Member States in order to become applicable law. Other EU regulatory instruments are also binding on Finland to the same extent as they are binding upon other Member States. The rulings of the European Court of Justice are also relevant because they are part of the body of EU law. Should there be a conflict between Finnish national legislation and EU law, the Finnish courts are under an obligation to give precedence to EU law.

[18] Finland is divided into a number of judicial districts, each with a district court. Civil and criminal cases are heard in district courts as the first judicial instance, including matters involving corporate law. In addition to the district courts, there are two levels of appeal: the regional appellate courts and the Supreme Court. Finnish law also allows parties to enter into agreements on alternative dispute resolution. Generally, parties to significant commercial agreements choose between arbitration provided by the Arbitration Act (967/1992, as amended) or the Rules of the Arbitration Institute of the Finland Chamber of Commerce. Also, the rules of international arbitration tribunals are used and enforceable in Finland.

[19] The Åland Islands are an autonomous part of Finland. Åland's laws are passed by the Provincial Parliament under the Act on the Autonomy of Åland. With regard to matters that are not legislated upon by the Provincial Parliament, the acts of the Parliament of Finland are valid in Åland.

1.4 Current Economic Aspects

[20] In 2021, the GDP in Finland was approximately EUR250 bn. The general government debt to GDP ratio at the end of 2021 was 65.8% and gross national income per capita was EUR46 416. The average inflation in 2021 was 2.2%.

[21] The Ministry of Finance of Finland estimated on 17 June 2022 that the gross domestic product (GDP) will grow by 1.4% in 2022. The invasion of Russia in Ukraine has affected the economic growth and caused a rise in the prices of energy, raw materials and food. As a consequence, the rise in the consumer prices is expected to decrease household purchasing power, consumption and economic growth. GDP growth will slow to 1.1% in 2023 and continue to grow moderately by 1.3% in 2024.

[22] The State of Finland has credit ratings from three credit rating agencies: Fitch Ratings, Moody's and Standard & Poor's. For long-term debt, they are currently AA+ with a stable outlook, Aa1 with stable outlook and AA+ with stable outlook, respectively. All three credit rating agencies affirmed the credit ratings of Finland in their latest reports made available in 2022.

[23] During the past few years, the deal-making activity in Finland has been on a relatively high level. By December 2021, Finland had reported 233 deals on Merger market for 2021. The number of deals and deal value in 2021 represented an increase in comparison with the data from 2020. However, the number of deals decreased slightly in comparison with 2018 and 2019 as well as the value of the deals decreased in comparison with 2018 and 2019. The most widely used payment type in corporate deals has traditionally been cash, although the use of shares or mixed consideration for deals is not uncommon.

[24] Generally, income per capita in Finland is among the highest in Western Europe and the country is celebrated for its generous welfare state. The Finnish welfare society, including healthcare, education, other necessary services and social security, are all funded primarily out of tax revenues.

1.5 Main Industries

[25] Until the end of the 1990s, the Finnish economy was heavily focused on the country's vast forests. Nokia Corporation subsequently came to symbolize the economic power of modern Finland, where telecommunications and technology have become the most important sectors. Although the importance of Nokia to the Finnish economy decreased over the years, the TMT sector continues to be important.

Finland is also known for its metals, engineering, electronics and mining industries.

[26] Finland derives about 40% of its GDP from exports. The main exports include electro-technical goods, metal products, machinery, wood and paper products and chemical industry products. The main imports include chemical industry products, metal products, machinery, transport equipment, electro-technical goods and mining industry products. In 2021, Finland's most significant export partners were Germany, Sweden and the United States, whereas Finland's most significant import partners were Germany, Sweden, Russia and China.

[27] The role of the Finnish state in the economy has decreased consistently over the past decades. The state played an important role in sponsoring economic development during the early years of the country's industrialization, but due to privatization and deregulation measures started in the early 1990s this role has diminished significantly. However, the state continues to own significant stakes in some large Finnish companies, many of which were state-owned companies before they were privatized. The role of the Finnish state in the economy is now focused on improving market efficiency and productivity rather than attempting to control individual companies.

1.6 Cultural Aspects

[28] From a business point of view, Finland can be accurately described as an open and welcoming place for foreign investment. Many large international corporations such as Microsoft, Google and Huawei have invested heavily in Finland by establishing R&D centres and other significant facilities in the country over the past decade.

[29] Although Finland is accommodating towards foreign investment, some aspects of the Nordic cultural heritage can be confusing to foreigners wishing to conduct business in the country. Generally speaking, it can be said that many Finns value tranquillity and avoid unnecessary small talk. Thus, short, to-the-point answers or other communication that can be seen as standoffish or blunt in some cultures should not be viewed as impolite when communicating with Finns. The business etiquette in Finland is characterized by placing a high value on clear communication and punctuality. A 'yes' means yes, and 'no' means no in the country. This, combined with a culture which admires modesty, can often lead Finns to under promise and over deliver on tasks. Gift giving is uncommon in business meetings, but small gifts may be exchanged after successful negotiations. The monetary value of such gifts should, however, be relatively low. The Finnish culture and society is also very egalitarian compared to many other cultures – students call their teachers by their first names and it is not uncommon to see politicians use public transportation. This informality and equality cover most aspects of Finnish life and can be especially puzzling to foreigners from countries with more pronounced social structures among different groups.

[30] The Nordic countries are often viewed as places of high taxation, which is sometimes seen as the main hindrance in doing business in the region. In reality, the corporate tax rate in Finland is just 20%, a comparatively low figure in the international context. Generally speaking, doing business in Finland is relatively free of political and economic risk with many international risk management companies rating the risk as negligible or low. Today the main risks involved in doing business in Finland are perhaps those related to the labour market. Relatively high costs of labour and a highly organized labour force are some of the main issues that investors should be aware of.

[31] Finland invests heavily in education. By the end of 2020, 74% of the population aged 15 or over had completed a post-comprehensive level qualification/ equivalent high school degree, and 32.6% of the population had completed a tertiary level qualification in 2020. Approximately 25% were without a post-comprehensive level qualification. Finland is also a top-performing country in terms of the quality of its educational system. The school system in Finland provides relatively equal access to high-quality education without tuition fees. In addition, as a result of the high-performing education system, English is widely spoken.

[32] In April 2022, 72.7% of people aged 15–64 in Finland had a paid job, compared with 70.1% in April 2021. Approximately 72.4% of men were in paid work, compared with 72.9% of women. In April 2022, the unemployment rate was 6.9%, compared with 9.6% during the previous year.

2 REGULATORY FRAMEWORK

2.1 Overview of Finnish Corporate Law

2.1.1 Laws, Regulations, Guidelines

[33] The primary source of corporate law in Finland is the Companies Act (624/ 2006, as amended), which governs limited liability companies. Separate legislation governs other forms of business: the Sole Proprietorship Act (128/1979, as amended), the Partnerships Act (389/1988, as amended) and the Co-Operatives Act (421/2013, as amended).

[34] Other relevant legislation includes the Sale of Goods Act (355/1987, as amended) and the Securities Market Act (746/2012, as amended). In addition, certain general principles of contract law such as the principles of freedom of contract, duty of loyalty and *pacta sunt servanda* are also applicable.

[35] Finnish contract law does not deviate in any material respect from that of any other civil law system within the EU, with German and Swedish civil law systems having had the strongest historical influence on the Finnish civil law system.

[36] Choice of law, jurisdiction and arbitration clauses are allowed under Finnish law and are binding between the parties. Council Regulation (EC) No. 44/2001

('Brussels I') is applicable in Finland and sets the rules regarding the determination of jurisdiction in cases involving multiple Member States.

2.1.2 Different Forms of Trade or Business

[37] The main options to carry on business in Finland are: (i) as a sole proprietor (sole trader or sole practitioner) (*yksityinen elinkeinonharjoittaja* or *toiminimi*), or (ii) through a specific organization which may be incorporated (i.e., a legal person) or unincorporated (i.e., an organization, which is not considered a legal person).

[38] Incorporated businesses may be further divided into two main groups: (i) companies (*yhtiö*), or (ii) cooperative societies (*osuuskunta*).

[39] Companies themselves may be further classified according to the following three categories:

(i) partnerships (*avoin yhtiö*);
(ii) limited partnerships (*kommandiittiyhtiö*); and
(iii) limited liability companies (*osakeyhtiö*), which may conduct business either as a public limited liability company (*julkinen osakeyhtiö*) or as a private limited liability company (*yksityinen osakeyhtiö*).

[40] Among these, limited liability companies are the most widely used corporate vehicle in Finland. These companies are seen as separate legal entities or legal persons. When it comes to 'hybrids' these have not been given any serious official consideration as to whether they should be regulated separately in the law. However, there is no prohibition on collaboration and especially large companies often organize some activities jointly through a legal person (equity joint ventures) or on a mere contractual basis (contractual joint ventures).

[41] A foreign company may also operate in Finland without setting up a company under Finnish company law by establishing a so-called branch office. An establishment of a branch office is subject to a commencement notification in the same manner as the establishment of other Finnish business entities. A branch office is, however, not a separate legal entity but acts for its parent company. If the foreign company is from a country outside the European Economic Area ('EEA'), it will also need a permit from the National Board of Patents and Registration for the establishment of a branch.

2.1.3 Limited Liability Company

General Principles of Limited Liability Companies

[42] The first chapter of the Companies Act enacts the main principles of a limited liability company. These general principles form the basis of the whole act and they must be used in the interpretation of the act. The principles are: (i) legal personality and the limited liability of shareholders, (ii) capital and its stability, (iii) the transferability of shares, (iv) the profit-generating purpose of a limited liability company, (v) the principle of majority rule, (vi) the principle of equal treatment, and (vii) fiduciary duties of the management and discretion of shareholders.

[43] The most important principles from a corporate governance point of view are the purpose of a limited liability company, the principle of equal treatment of shareholders and the management's duty of care. The purpose of a limited liability company is to generate profits for its shareholders, unless otherwise provided in the articles of association. According to the principle of equal treatment, all shares shall carry the same rights in the company unless otherwise provided in the articles of association. No decisions can be made or other measures taken that unjustly benefit a shareholder or another person at the expense of the company or another shareholder.

[44] Pursuant to the Companies Act, the management of a company has an obligation to act carefully (duty of care) and promote the best interests of the company. The obligation to promote the best interests of the company usually corresponds to promoting the business of the company and, indirectly, the interests of the shareholders as a group. In addition to the duty of care and the obligation to promote the best interests of the company, the management must seek to ensure the equal treatment of all shareholders, and each member of the board of directors must comply with the conflict of interest provisions (duty of loyalty).

Public and Private Limited Liability Companies

[45] Under the Companies Act, limited liability companies can be either public or private companies. The main difference between public and private companies is that only the securities of a public company may be admitted to public trading governed by the Securities Market Act. Also, certain provisions in the Companies Act are only applicable to public companies.

Incorporation

[46] A limited liability company can be established by one or more founding shareholders (who can be either legal entities or private individuals) upon the execution of a written incorporation agreement signed by all founding shareholders. By signing the incorporation agreement, a shareholder subscribes for such quantity of shares as indicated in the incorporation agreement.

[47] The minimum contents of the incorporation agreement include:

(i) the date of entry of the incorporation agreement;
(ii) the names of all shareholders and the number of shares subscribed for by each of them;
(iii) the subscription price;
(iv) the date when the subscription price is to be paid; and
(v) the members of the company's board of directors.

[48] The company's articles of association must be attached to the incorporation agreement. The minimum contents of the articles of association include:

(i) the company's trade name;

(ii) the municipality in Finland in which the company has its registered office; and
(iii) the company's field(s) of operation.

[49] As a general principle, all shares have equal rights in the company. However, a company can state in its articles of association that the company has or can have different classes of shares with different rights or obligations. Shares belong to different classes when they: (i) differ from each other as regards voting rights or rights in relation to the distribution of the assets of the company, or (ii) are otherwise designated in the articles of association as belonging to different classes. There is no minimum share capital requirement for a private company, but the minimum share capital of a public company is EUR80 000. A private limited liability company may be established without share capital or with share capital. As a rule, the subscription price of a share is to be credited to the share capital, unless provided in the incorporation agreement or the articles of association that part of the subscription price is to be credited to the reserve for invested unrestricted equity, or unless otherwise provided in the Accounting Act (1336/1997, as amended).

[50] A subscription price paid in cash is to be paid into an account of the company in a Finnish deposit bank or in a branch of a foreign credit institution licensed to accept deposits in Finland or into a comparable foreign account. If the subscription price is paid in full or in part with other assets (contribution in kind), the assets must at the time of conveyance have financial value to the company at least equal to the price thus paid. An undertaking to perform work or services may not be used as a contribution in kind. Any provisions on the payment of the subscription price in kind must be included in the incorporation agreement. The subscription price, whether in cash or in kind, must be fully paid prior to the notification of the company's establishment to the Finnish Trade Register.

[51] Shareholders' agreements are commonly used instruments, which enable contractual arrangements regarding certain matters agreed upon by shareholders of a limited liability company. Excluding the non-dispositive matters provided for in the Companies Act, the shareholders are free to agree upon any other matters concerning the limited liability company as they wish. A shareholders' agreement entered into by the shareholders would typically govern such dispositive matters. A breach of a shareholders' agreement has consequences in contract law among the parties, such as an obligation to pay contractual damages, but not under corporate law, which is assessed independently. A shareholders' agreement would bind only the parties to it and, consequently, it could not be relied upon in claims against any third parties, the company itself included, unless the company is also party to the shareholders' agreement.

Registration with the Finnish Trade Register

[52] A limited liability company becomes fully incorporated upon registration with the Finnish Trade Register, which forms a part of the Finnish Patent and Registration Office. The company must notify the Finnish Trade Register for registration within three months of the signing of the incorporation agreement, at the failure of which the incorporation would lapse. The company is incorporated on the date on

which it is registered with the Finnish Trade Register. Documents and forms submitted to the Finnish Patent and Registration Office must be in Finnish or Swedish. In special cases, documents in English may be accepted.

Tax Registration

[53] Usually, a company can be registered in the Tax Register by using the same form as for incorporation. Filing such start-up notification form will result in the company's entry into the register of VAT-liable businesses, employers, or persons liable for paying tax on insurance premiums, or the prepayment register of taxpayers.

[54] The obligation to register depends on the nature of the business operation. For example, a company may not need to become VAT registered if the company is not deemed to have a permanent establishment in Finland. Further, if a company has no permanent establishment in Finland for income tax purposes, it does not have to seek entry in the Register of Employers. However, submitting the start-up notification form will always result in registration in the records maintained by the Finnish Tax Administration.

Financial Reporting Requirements

[55] Finnish corporate law includes extensive reporting requirements for limited liability companies. All such companies are subject to an accounting obligation and must prepare annual accounts at the end of each accounting period and file them with the Finnish Trade Register within six months of the end of each accounting period.

[56] In addition to the annual accounts, which include key performance figures of the company, such as the income statement, an annual report must also be published by listed companies. The requirements for the annual documents are listed in the Auditing Act (1141/2015, as amended), which follows standards set by EU legislation. Applying the International Financial Reporting Standards (IFRS) is also mandatory for listed companies.

[57] The Companies Act (624/2006, as amended) also contains provisions on public notices a company must send in the event of changes affecting the company. Generally, a public notice must be sent out to the creditors of the company in the event of a merger, demerger or reduction of share capital. Public notices serve as an invitation for creditors to be heard on issues regarding their outstanding accounts receivable.

[58] The Securities Market Act (746/2012, as amended) contains disclosure obligations regarding securities issued by listed companies. In the act, these are divided into information that must be disclosed either periodically or on an ongoing basis. Information regarding the issuer's financial reporting must be released periodically. The ongoing disclosure obligation includes information, which could materially affect the value of the company's shares. The details of the ongoing disclosure obligation are included in Regulation (EU) No. 596/2014 of the European Parliament and of the Council on market abuse ('Market Abuse Regulation').

Corporate Structure

General Meeting

[59] The shareholders exercise their decision-making power at the general meeting. The ordinary general meeting must be held within six months of the end of each financial year. In addition to being physically present in a meeting place, the shareholders can also use their decision-making power by means of data communication systems and technical equipment. Meetings can also be held without a physical meeting place, i.e., fully online.

[60] Pursuant to the Companies Act, the following decisions must be made at the ordinary general meeting:

(i) adoption of the financial statements, which in a parent company also means the adoption of the consolidated financial statements;
(ii) use of the profit shown on the balance sheet;
(iii) whether to discharge from liability the members of the board of directors, the members of the supervisory board and the managing director;
(iv) election and compensation of the members of the board of directors and the members of the supervisory board, and the election of the auditor, unless it is otherwise provided in the Companies Act or the company's articles of association on their term or election; and
(v) other matters that, according to the company's articles of association, are to be decided by the ordinary general meeting.

[61] An extraordinary general meeting can be held as and when necessary. However, an extraordinary general meeting must be held in the following circumstances:

(i) when required by the company's articles of association;
(ii) the board of directors considers it necessary;
(iii) a shareholder or an auditor demands the same in accordance with the Companies Act; or
(iv) the supervisory board considers it necessary and has competence, under the articles of association, to call an extraordinary general meeting.

[62] According to the implemented Shareholder Rights Directive ((EU) 2017/828, 'SHRD II'), the board of directors shall present a remuneration policy to the general meeting of shareholders of a listed company at the time of every material change and in any case at least every four years. The general meeting shall decide whether it will support the policy or not. However, the shareholders' decision shall be an advisory vote. If the general meeting rejects the policy, a revised policy is required to be presented at the next annual general meeting.

[63] Furthermore, listed companies are required to resolve upon the approval of the remuneration report in the annual general meeting. The decision shall be an advisory vote.

[64] The Companies Act does not stipulate any specific quorum for the general meeting. Consequently, unless otherwise stipulated in the articles of association, one shareholder may constitute a quorum.

[65] A unanimous vote of shareholders may make a decision without holding a meeting in a matter within the competence of the general meeting. The decision must be written down, dated, numbered and signed. If the company has more than one shareholder, at least two of them must sign the decision. In other respects, the provisions on the minutes of the general meeting apply to such written decision.

[66] When an actual meeting is held, a proposal that has been supported by more than half of the votes cast shall constitute a decision of the general meeting, unless it is otherwise provided in the Companies Act.

[67] If a decision must be made by a qualified majority, a proposal that has been supported by at least two-thirds of the votes cast and the shares represented at the meeting shall constitute a decision.

[68] Unless it is otherwise provided in the Companies Act or the articles of association, the following decisions shall be made by a qualified majority:

(i) amendments to the articles of association;
(ii) directed share issues;
(iii) issue of option rights and other special rights entitling to shares;
(iv) acquisition and redemption of own shares in a public company;
(v) directed acquisition of own shares;
(vi) mergers;
(vii) demergers; and
(viii) liquidation and the termination of liquidation.

[69] The requirement to have a qualified majority may not be relieved in the articles of association.

[70] In an election of the members of the board of directors and auditors, the person receiving the most votes is elected. The general meeting may decide before the election that the person receiving more than half the votes cast shall be elected. In the event of a tie, an election is decided by drawing lots or, in another voting situation, the tie-breaking vote is cast by the chairperson, unless it is otherwise provided in the articles of association. The requirement of a majority may be relieved by way of the articles of association only with regard to elections.

Board of Directors

[71] Pursuant to the Companies Act, a limited liability company must have a board of directors consisting of one to five regular members, unless otherwise provided in the articles of association. If there are fewer than three members, at least one deputy member must be elected. If there are several members of the board of directors, they must elect a chairman from among them.

[72] The general meeting elects the members of the board of directors, unless it is provided in the articles of association that the supervisory board is to appoint the members. A member of the board of directors may be dismissed prior to the conclusion of a term by the body that appointed such member.

[73] Pursuant to the Companies Act, the members of the board of directors are under an obligation to act with due care and promote the best interests of the company. The board of directors represents the company and sees to the administration of the company and the appropriate organization of its operations (general competence). The board of directors is responsible for delegating responsibility over the management of the company accounts and finances. The board of directors or its members must not comply with a decision of the general meeting, the supervisory board or the board of directors where it is contrary to the Companies Act or the articles of association of the company.

Managing Director

[74] While the board of directors is a mandatory corporate body, it is optional for a limited liability company to have a managing director. If a managing director is appointed, he or she represents the company in matters falling within the managing director's duties, which include the following:

(i) responsibility over the executive management of the company in accordance with the instructions and orders given by the board of directors (general competence);
(ii) responsibility over the accounts of the company ensuring that they are in compliance with the law and that the company's financial affairs have been arranged in a reliable manner; and
(iii) responsibility over supplying the members of the board of directors with the information necessary for the performance of their duties as directors.

Supervisory Board

[75] Pursuant to the Companies Act, a limited liability company may have a supervisory board composed of at least three members of which one has to be a chairperson. However, in practice, it is rare for Finnish companies to have a supervisory board. The supervisory board supervises the administration of the company, which is the responsibility of the board of directors and the managing director. The managing director or a member of the board of directors in Finland cannot be a member of the supervisory board.

Auditor

[76] The general meeting elects an auditor to examine the company's annual accounts to ensure their authenticity and compliance with the Companies Act and the Auditing Act. There is no obligation to elect an auditor for a company where not more than one of the following conditions was met in both the latest completed financial year and the financial year immediately preceding it:

(i) the balance sheet total exceeds EUR100 000;
(ii) net sales or comparable revenue exceeds EUR200 000; or
(iii) the average number of employees exceeds three.

[77] An auditor has to be always elected for companies whose principal activities consist of owning and holding securities and for companies which exercise significant influence over the operating and financial policies of another entity that is obliged to keep accounting records. At least one of the auditors elected by the general meeting has to be an authorized public accountant or a firm of authorized public accountants if the company is a public-interest company or if at least two of the following conditions were met in the latest completed financial year:

(i) the balance sheet total exceeds EUR25 000 000;
(ii) net sales or comparable revenue exceeds EUR50 000 000; or
(iii) the average number of employees exceeds 300.

Management's Liability

[78] Members of the board of directors and the supervisory board and the managing director are liable for the loss that they, in violation of the management's duty of care, have deliberately or negligently caused to the company. Such persons are likewise liable for the loss that they, in violation of other provisions of the Companies Act or the articles of association, have deliberately or negligently caused to the company, a shareholder or a third party.

[79] If the loss has been caused by a violation of the Companies Act, other than by a violation of the general principles set out in Chapter 1 of such act, or if the loss has been caused by a breach of the provisions of the articles of association, it is deemed to have been caused negligently, insofar as the person liable does not prove that he or she has acted with due care. The same provision applies to loss that has been caused by an act to the benefit of a related party.

Shareholders

[80] A limited liability company is a legal person distinct from its shareholders. The shareholders have no personal liability for the obligations of the company.

[81] The shareholders are obliged to pay up the subscription price of the subscribed shares. The board of directors may declare the right to a share forfeited if the subscription price, together with any possible overdue interest thereon, has not been paid by the due date and the board of directors has not granted an extension to the subscriber.

Authority of Shareholders and Board of Directors

[82] As a general rule, the general meeting of shareholders is authorized to make decisions in matters which have been defined to fall within its scope of authority in the Companies Act and/or the articles of association. Certain matters, as defined in the Companies Act, are solely for the general meeting to decide upon. However, it is possible that, pursuant to the articles of association, the general meeting may also be authorized to decide upon matters which fall within the general competence of the board of directors or the managing director.

[83] Further, the board of directors may refer a matter which would otherwise fall within its general powers or the duties of the managing director to the attention of the general meeting. This does not require any explicit provisions in the articles of association.

[84] The general meeting is not obliged to make decisions on matters, which fall within the general powers of the board of directors or the managing director if such matters have been delegated to the general meeting by the board of directors. In such a situation, the liability attached to such decision-making remains with the board of directors. Nevertheless, the general meeting may not refuse to decide upon matters which have been referred to it in the articles of association.

Representation

[85] Pursuant to the Companies Act, a company can be represented by virtue of position or rank in the company or designation. The former applies to the members of the board of directors or the managing director when the articles of association provide them with such representative rights. The latter comes into effect when the board of directors grants this right to a member or members of the board, the managing director or some other designated person, in which case the right to represent the company is personal and not subject to position or rank. Companies can also appoint representatives to act *per procurationem*.

Minority-Shareholder Rights

[86] The principle of equal treatment of shareholders is one of the leading principles of the Companies Act. No corporate decision, which would grant unjust benefit to a shareholder or other party at the expense of another shareholder, can be made at a general meeting or by the board of directors or management of the company. A corporate decision made at a general meeting that violates this principle could be objected by minority shareholders. Corporate resolutions made by the board of directors or management that violate the principle may subject the directors and/or officers of the company to liability for damages.

General Meeting

[87] An extraordinary general meeting shall be held, if an auditor or shareholders with at least 10% of all shares, or a smaller proportion as provided in the articles of association, so demand in writing in order for a given matter to be dealt with. Also, such shareholder shall have the right to have a matter falling within the competence of the general meeting dealt with by the general meeting, if the shareholder so demands in writing from the board of directors well in advance of the meeting, so that the matter can be mentioned in the notice for the meeting.

Right to Redeem Minority Shares

[88] According to the Companies Act, a majority shareholder with more than 90% of the shares and votes can redeem the shares owned by the minority shareholders. If this threshold is not met, the right to redeem does not exist. Correspondingly, in such circumstances, the minority shareholders can demand the majority shareholder to redeem such shares.

[89] In calculating the 90% threshold, shares owned by the company itself or by its subsidiaries, or voting restrictions included in law or in the articles of association of the company are not taken into account. In addition, the redemption right (or obligation) can arise not only through directly held shares but also from indirect shareholdings. According to the Companies Act, the shares and voting rights of controlled corporate entities or foundations are taken into account when calculating the 90% threshold.

[90] The redemption right (or obligation) relates to shares and does not directly apply to any warrants or other special rights granted by the company. However, the terms and conditions of such rights must include provisions on the status of such rights in connection with the redemption of minority shareholders. Therefore, it is possible that the terms and conditions of warrants or other special rights stipulate that such instruments must be redeemed simultaneously with shares. In the absence of such provision, the majority shareholder does not have a right (or obligation) to redeem the warrants and/or other special rights.

[91] Any disputes concerning the redemption right or the redemption price are resolved by arbitrators appointed by the Finnish Central Chamber of Commerce in accordance with Chapter 18 of the Companies Act. In the case of broadly held listed companies, the commencement of arbitration proceedings, together with the appointment of a trustee to represent passive minority shareholders, is the only practicable way of completing a full redemption of all shares held by minority shareholders. In the event, arbitration proceedings to establish the redemption price are being held in circumstances where the right of redemption has been legally established (i.e., a holding exceeding 90%) and the majority shareholder seeking redemption has posted acceptable security (bank guarantee) for the payment of the redemption price, arbitrators will typically issue an interim order confirming that the title to the shares subject to redemption is deemed to have transferred to the majority shareholder.

Annual Accounts and Right to Demand Appointment of Auditor or Special Audit

[92] According to the Companies Act, decisions of the general meeting regarding approval of the accounts, use of profits and discharge from liability must be postponed to an extraordinary general meeting of shareholders held at a later date if minority shareholders that own at least 10% of the shares of the company so demand.

[93] According to the Companies Act, if minority shareholders that own at least 10% of the shares in the company or one-third of the shares represented at the ordinary general meeting so demand at a general meeting, and if a company does not have an auditor pursuant to law or articles of association, an auditor must be appointed to the company.

[94] In addition, minority shareholders that own at least 10% of the shares of the company or one-third of the shares represented at the ordinary general meeting can demand at the ordinary general meeting that a special audit of the company be conducted by an outside auditor. In such case, a shareholder may apply to the Regional State Administrative Agency of the place where the company has its registered office for an order of a special audit of the administration and accounts of the company for a given past period or for given measures or circumstances.

Financial Rights

[95] At least one-half of the profits of the financial period, out of which the amounts not to be distributed under the articles of association have been deducted, must be distributed as dividend if a demand to this effect is made at the ordinary general meeting by shareholders that own at least 10% of the shares in the company before the decision on the use of the profits has been made. However, a shareholder may not demand the distribution of profits in excess of the amount that can be distributed in the absence of consent by the creditors, nor in excess of 8% of the equity of the company. Any distributions of profits already made during the financial period and before the ordinary general meeting would have to be subtracted from the amount to be distributed.

[96] Also, other provisions on the minority dividend may be included in the articles of association. The right to the minority dividend may be restricted only by the consent of all shareholders.

Litigation and Claims

[97] Shareholders can, in their own name and at their own expense, file claims to nullify any decision of the general meeting or to claim damages from the company's directors, officers, auditors and other shareholders. In addition, even when the general meeting has approved a proposal to discharge the company's management from liability or another proposal not to claim damages from the company's directors, officers, auditors or other shareholders, minority shareholders who own at least 10% of the shares of the company and have voted against such proposal can claim damages from the above persons on behalf, and at the expense, of the company (derivative claim).

Distribution of Assets

[98] The assets of the company may be distributed to the shareholders only as provided in the Companies Act by:

(i) distribution of profits (dividend) and the distribution of assets from reserves of unrestricted equity;
(ii) reduction of the share capital;
(iii) acquisition and redemption of own shares; and
(iv) dissolution and deregistration of the company.

[99] The distribution of assets must be based on the latest audited financial statements. Any material changes in the financial position of the company after the date of the financial statements must be taken into account in the distribution. If it is known or should be known at the time of a distribution that the company is insolvent or that the distribution will cause the insolvency of the company, no distribution shall be permitted.

[100] The amount of a company's own shares available for purchase is limited to 10% in public limited liability companies. For a private limited liability company, there are no such restrictions.

Liquidation

General

[101] In Finnish legal terminology, liquidation means a voluntary winding up or dissolution of a company. The purpose of the liquidation process under the Companies Act is to clarify the financial status of the company, sell the company's remaining assets, pay the company's debts and distribute any excess funds to the shareholders, after which the company is considered dissolved.

General Meeting Resolving upon Liquidation

[102] The only competent company body to decide upon liquidation is the general meeting. In conjunction with its resolution to place the company into liquidation, the general meeting must also elect one or more liquidators to replace the company's board of directors and the managing director.

[103] In order for the shareholders to pass a resolution to place the company into liquidation, the resolution must be supported by: (i) shareholders that represent at least two-thirds of the votes cast in the meeting and of the shares represented in the meeting, and (ii) shareholders that represent at least two-thirds of each series of shares represented in the meeting.

Liquidation Process

[104] After the general meeting, the liquidator must file a registration statement with the Finnish Trade Register for purposes of registering the liquidation status of the company and his/her own role as a liquidator.

[105] The liquidator must sell all the assets of the company and pay the company's debts. The liquidator must also apply for a public summons directed to all the creditors of the company. The public summons must contain information about all the known creditors. The purpose of the summons is to discover any unknown creditors of the company and must be published no later than three months before the date on which unknown creditors must make a claim. A copy of the summons is sent to the known creditors. Any unknown claims not presented by the due date will extinguish on the due date.

[106] If considered necessary, the liquidator may also prepare financial statements for the period preceding liquidation. However, typically, the financial statements would be prepared only if the general meeting so decides or if the liquidator otherwise considers the preparation of financial statements to be necessary or advisable. If prepared, the financial statements need to be audited.

[107] It is the obligation of the liquidator to ensure that all the debts of the company are paid. If the company's liabilities exceed its assets and all its debts cannot be paid, the liquidator must place the company into bankruptcy. In order to avoid bankruptcy, the liquidator would need to ensure that the company has no outstanding liabilities.

[108] After all the liabilities have been satisfied (or waived) and, if relevant, any remaining funds distributed to the shareholders, the liquidator must prepare the final liquidation accounts by preparing a report of the entire liquidation process, including a description of the distribution of the company's excess funds. The report, together with the relevant annexes, must be provided to the company's auditor, who shall within one month thereof issue an auditor's statement concerning the final liquidation accounts and liquidation administration.

[109] After all such steps have been completed, the liquidator would invite the shareholders to a general meeting for purposes of examining the final liquidation accounts. The final liquidation accounts are approved by a simple majority. The company is considered dissolved after the final liquidation accounts have been approved in the general meeting. The liquidator must also, without delay, submit the necessary forms to the Finnish Trade Register for registering the company as dissolved. The final liquidation accounts must be registered with the Finnish Trade Register within two months after having been approved by the general meeting.

2.1.4 Private Acquisitions

Share Purchase and Business Transfer

[110] A private acquisition can be made either by a purchase of shares or by a purchase of all or a part of the business of a privately held limited liability company. While in the purchase of shares, all the assets and liabilities of the target company will remain with the target company, in the purchase of assets, the parties can, in principle, freely decide upon which assets and liabilities will be acquired. In the latter case, the parties often also agree on the continuation of the transferred business by the acquirer.

[111] There is no specific legislation applicable to the acquisitions of privately held companies in Finland. In addition to general principles of contract law, the main legislation in this context is found in the Sale of Goods Act, the Companies Act, the Securities Market Act and other corporate law.

Due Diligence Review

[112] Prior to any private acquisition, as well as in connection with any M&A transaction, the acquirer normally conducts a due diligence investigation of the target company and its business, in particular concentrating on assessing such risks and liabilities that are not apparent in the financial statements or other publicly available material on the target company. The acquirer, pursuant to the caveat emptor principle, carries the risk of not properly investigating the target company. Except for certain provisions of the Companies Act, mainly on mergers, Finnish legislation contains no direct rules on due diligence. Due diligence is an internationally established procedure in business, including in Finland, which safeguards shareholder interests.

Acquisition Agreement

[113] There are no requirements under Finnish law as to the form of acquisition agreement, except where real estate is being transferred, which requires the agreement to be in writing and signed in the presence of a notary public (unless the agreement is signed electronically in the Property Transaction Service provided by the Finnish National Land Survey). Acquisition agreements typically follow the framework of Anglo-Saxon business culture.

Financial Assistance and Security Interests

[114] In Finland, acquisitions are often financed by bank loans provided by either domestic or Nordic banks and in the case of larger deals, international banks are also often involved. The Companies Act places certain restrictions on financial assistance and forbids limited liability companies from providing loans, assets or security for the purpose of a third party acquiring shares in the company or its parent company. This rule does not, however, apply when the purpose is to acquire shares for employees of the company.

[115] Finnish law recognizes most types of assets as eligible to be used as security. Generally, assets which: (i) can be individually identified, (ii) have monetary value and (iii) are freely transferable qualify as security. The Act on Enterprise Mortgage (634/1984, as amended) contains provisions on the use of floating charges, which are often referred to by the term 'enterprise mortgage' (*yrityskiinnitys*) in Finland. Floating charges are available for movable assets only and a floating charge application must be filed with, and approved by, the Finnish Patent and Registration Office in order to be valid. The Restructuring of Enterprises Act (47/1993, as amended) sets the rules on debt arrangements in case of an insolvency. The priority of claims as per the Act on Ranking of Claims (1578/1992, as amended) is as follows: (i) secured claims, (ii) claims arising in connection with reorganization, (iii) floating charge (50% of the value of the mortgage), and (iv) unsecured claims in proportion to the amount of the debt.

Mergers and Demergers

Mergers

[116] *General*: A legal merger (through absorption) results in the dissolution of the merging company (or merging companies) and the transfer of all of its (or their) assets and liabilities to the surviving company in a so-called universal succession. The surviving company receives the full legal position of the merging company in respect of transferred assets and liabilities.

[117] *Merger Consideration:* As a general rule, a merger requires that the shareholders of the merging company receive a merger consideration as compensation for giving up their shareholding in the merging company. As an exception to this rule, no merger consideration is paid in respect of any shares in the merging company owned by the surviving company (parent-subsidiary merger).

[118] According to the Companies Act, the general assumption is that the shareholders of the merging company are given the opportunity to continue as the shareholders of the surviving company and, thus, would receive shares in the surviving company as merger consideration. However, as long as the shareholders of the merging company are being treated equally, the merger consideration can also consist of cash, other assets or future undertakings, such as debt instruments, or a combination thereof. Further, pursuant to the Companies Act, the merger consideration to the shareholders of a merging company can also be given by some other party than the surviving company, generally being the surviving company's parent company (triangular merger).

[119] *Merger Process*: The merger process is a statutory process set forth in the Companies Act. The merger process (excluding the preparation of the final accounts) generally takes from four to eight months, with six months being the approximate average time for a merger of Finnish companies. Also, the preparation of the merger plan takes some time depending on the circumstances of each individual case.

[120] The merger process includes the following seven main steps:

1. Merger Plan

[121] A merger process is commenced by the board of directors of the merging company and the surviving company together executing a merger plan. The Companies Act sets forth the minimum requirements for the contents of the merger plan, and it must include all information which is relevant to the shareholders and creditors of the merging and surviving companies in evaluating the merger.

[122] For a merger through absorption, the merger plan must include, *inter alia*:

(i) a clarification on the purpose of, and the grounds for, the merger;
(ii) a proposal for merger consideration to the shareholders of the merging company;
(iii) an account, or a proposal on the rights, of warrant holders, or holders of special rights entitling to shares, of the merging company;
(iv) an account of the assets, liabilities and equity of the merging company and of circumstances relevant to the valuation thereof;
(v) the intended effect of the merger on the balance sheet of the surviving company and accounting principles applicable to the merger; and
(vi) a proposal for the effective date of registration of the merger (non-binding).

[123] After the merger plan has been executed by the relevant boards of directors, an auditor must issue a statement on the merger plan prior to its registration. Such an auditor can be the auditor of either the merging or the surviving company or any third-party auditor. In practice, the auditor for this purpose is agreed and appointed in the merger plan. In its statement, the authorized auditor must assess whether accurate and fair information has been presented in the merger plan as a basis for determining the merger consideration and distribution of such consideration.

2. Registration of Merger Plan

[124] The merger plan must be registered with the Finnish Trade Register within one month from its execution. In connection with the registration, the Finnish Trade Register will examine whether the merger plan complies with the Companies Act and whether the registration of the merger plan is timely.

3. Creditor Hearing Process

[125] The merging company must apply for a public announcement to its creditors by the Finnish Trade Register within four months after the registration of the merger plan. (The surviving company must also apply for a public announcement if the auditor has in its statement stated that the merger may endanger the payment of any debts of the surviving company.) The public announcement will give such creditors, whose receivables have arisen prior to the registration of the merger plan, the opportunity to oppose the merger.

[126] Furthermore, pursuant to the Companies Act, the company must also notify in writing, at least one month prior to the due date mentioned in the public announcement, all those known creditors whose receivables have arisen prior to the registration of the merger plan.

[127] As such, merger proceedings do not result in premature payment of the debts of the merging company. However, if a creditor opposes the merger, the receivables of the creditor must be paid or a sufficient security placed to secure the payment of the creditor's receivables, and generally, such a solution must be reached within one month after the due date mentioned in the public announcement.

4. Approval of Merger

[128] The merger must be approved by both the merging and the surviving company within four months after the registration of the merger plan. If the merger is not approved without changes, the merger is aborted.

[129] In the merging company, a general meeting of shareholders must be convened to approve the merger. The merger is approved by the general meeting with a majority of two-thirds of votes cast and shares represented in the meeting (and, if there are different share classes, also two-thirds of shares of each share class represented in the meeting).

[130] In the surviving company, the board of directors approves the merger. However, if shareholders holding at least 5% of all shares in the company so demand, the merger must be approved in a general meeting of shareholders. The shareholders need to be informed of the merger in the same manner as a general meeting is convened.

5. Possible Redemption

[131] The shareholders (and possibly also any holders of warrants and other special rights) of the merging company can, in the general meeting of shareholders that resolves upon the merger, demand the redemption of their shares for cash. If the redemption cannot be agreed with the surviving company, the dispute regarding the redemption (including the appropriate redemption price, which must equal the 'fair price' of the shares) will be settled in arbitration proceedings. Such arbitration proceedings should not, however, have any effect on the duration of the merger process as the shareholders only have the right to the redemption price after the dispute is submitted into arbitration.

6. Execution of Merger

[132] The merger enters into force when the execution of the merger has been registered with the Finnish Trade Register. The execution of the merger must be applied for with the Finnish Trade Register within six months from the resolutions approving the merger. The execution of the merger can only be applied for after the period of the public announcement has elapsed and either no creditor has opposed the merger or the receivables of any opposing creditors have been settled or secured by a sufficient security. The execution of the merger further requires a statement from the auditor confirming that the surviving company receives full coverage for any amount added to its equity in the merger.

7. Final Financial Accounts

[133] The final financial accounts of the merging company, up to the date of execution of the merger, must be prepared (and usually also audited) as soon as possible after the execution of the merger. Thereafter, irrespective of the fact that the merging company has already been dissolved by the execution of the merger, the board of directors of the merging company must convene a meeting of the shareholders of the merging company, who must approve the final accounts. The final accounts must be filed for registration with the Finnish Trade Register within two months from the approval of the final accounts by the shareholders of the merging company.

2.1.5 Cross-Border Mergers

[134] *General*: The 'Cross-Border Merger Directive' (Directive 2005/56/EC of the European Parliament and of the Council of 26 October 2005 on cross-border mergers of limited liability companies, as amended) was implemented in Finland in December 2007. The implementation of the Cross-Border Merger Directive enables cross-border mergers of Finnish limited liability companies and foreign entities. Further, as an EU member state, Finland is required to implement directive (EU) 2019/2121 of the European Parliament and of the Council of 27 November 2019 amending Directive (EU) 2017/1132 as regards cross-border conversions, mergers and divisions by 31 January 2023 which will update the cross-border merger process as well as create rules for cross-border conversions and divisions.

[135] *Merger Process*: The discussion below relates solely to the merger process in connection with cross-border mergers where a Finnish limited liability company merges into a foreign entity, which fulfils the requirements set forth in the Cross-Border Merger Directive.

[136] Generally speaking, the merger process in a cross-border merger is the same as in a national merger. There are, however, certain differences in the procedures, relating mainly to the nature of cross-border mergers involving two or more jurisdictions. For example, in addition to the contents of the merger plan, the merger plan needs to include, *inter alia*:

(i) information on the registers to which the parties to the merger have been registered;

(ii) clarification on implications of the merger to employment matters and on employee participation; and
(iii) procedures to protect and ensure employees' rights of participation in the surviving company.

[137] As in a Finnish merger, the merger plan will need to be registered with the Finnish Trade Register and the Finnish procedures regarding the protection of creditors will apply.

[138] Also, as in a Finnish merger, the execution of the merger must be applied for by the Finnish merging company from the Finnish Trade Register within six months from the date of the resolutions approving the merger. As a general rule, the permission to execute the merger will be granted if there are no opposing creditors (or such creditors have received payment of a sufficient security for their receivables) and if sufficient clarification on employee participation in the surviving company has been delivered to the Finnish Trade Register in accordance with the Cross-Border Merger Directive. As a condition for the execution of the merger, foreign limited liability companies will have to adopt the merger plan, relevant provisions of the Companies Act, such as the right of redemption, as well as the rules regarding employee representation in European Companies (SE) and European Cooperative Societies (SCE), when applicable.

[139] After granting permission to execute the merger, the Finnish Trade Register will issue a certificate regarding the granted permission, in accordance with the Cross-Border Merger Directive. The certificate must be delivered to the applicable registration authority in respect of the surviving company within six months from the issuance of the certificate.

[140] The cross-border merger will become effective in accordance with laws applicable to the surviving company. Thereafter, the applicable registration authority in respect of the surviving company will issue a notification to the Finnish Trade Register, which will delete the Finnish merged company from the Finnish Trade Register. If the registration is intended to take effect on a certain fixed date, it is advisable to contact the Finnish Trade Register in advance to discuss the possibility of implementing the merger on such date. After the registration of the merger and the deletion of the Finnish company from the Finnish Trade Register, the merger cannot be declared invalid.

[141] *Employee Participation:* If a party in a cross-border merger has an employee participation scheme in the administration of the company, a specific negotiation group must be convened to discuss the employees' participation with the parties in the cross-border merger. Such negotiation group can give its statement regarding the merger plan, and this statement must also be presented to the shareholders. In Finland, employee participation in a merger process only applies to companies with more than 150 employees.

2.1.6 Demergers

[142] *General*: A company can demerge either through a full demerger or a partial demerger. In a full demerger, all assets and liabilities of the demerging company are transferred to two or more receiving companies, and the demerging company is dissolved. In a partial demerger, a part of the liabilities and assets of the demerging company is transferred to a receiving company and the demerging company continues its existence after the completion of the partial demerger. In a partial demerger, the demerging company continues its operations and no ownership change occurs in respect of the continuing company's assets and liabilities. However, in a partial demerger, only such liabilities that relate to the demerged assets are transferred to the receiving company.

[143] *Demerger Consideration:* In a demerger, the shareholders of the demerging company receive a demerger consideration as compensation for giving up their shareholding in the demerging company.

[144] According to the Companies Act, the general assumption is that the shareholders of the demerging company are given the opportunity to continue as the shareholders of the receiving company or companies and, thus, would receive shares in the receiving company or companies as demerger consideration. However, as long as the shareholders of the demerging company are being treated equally, the demerger consideration can also consist of cash, other assets or future undertakings, such as debt instruments, or a combination thereof.

[145] *Demerger Process*: The demerger process is a statutory process set forth in the Companies Act. The demerger process (excluding the preparation of the final accounts) generally takes from four to eight months, with six months being the approximate average time for a demerger of Finnish companies. Also, the preparation of the demerger plan takes some time depending on the circumstances of each individual case.

[146] The demerger process includes the following seven main steps:

1. Demerger Plan

[147] A demerger process is commenced by the board of directors of the demerging company and the receiving company or companies together executing a demerger plan. The Companies Act sets forth the minimum requirements for the contents of the demerger plan and it must include, among other things: (i) the proposed demerger consideration, (ii) an account of the assets, liabilities and equity of the demerging company and matters affecting their valuation, and (iii) a proposal for the distribution of assets and liabilities to the receiving company/companies.

[148] After the demerger plan has been executed by the relevant boards of directors, an auditor must issue a statement on the demerger plan prior to its registration. Such auditor can be the auditor of either the demerging or the receiving company or any third-party auditor. In practice, the auditor for this purpose is agreed and appointed in the demerger plan. In its statement, the authorized auditor must assess whether accurate and fair information has been presented in the demerger plan as a basis for determining the demerger consideration and distribution of such consideration.

2. Registration of Demerger Plan

[149] The demerger plan must be registered with the Finnish Trade Register within one month from its execution. In connection with the registration, the Finnish Trade Register will examine whether the demerger plan complies with the Companies Act and whether the registration of the demerger plan is timely.

3. Creditor Hearing Process

[150] The demerging company must apply for a public announcement to its creditors by the Finnish Trade Register within four months after the registration of the demerger plan. (The receiving company or companies must also apply for a public announcement if the auditor has in its statement stated that the demerger may endanger the payment of any debts of the receiving company.) The public announcement will give such creditors, whose receivables have arisen prior to the registration of the demerger plan, the opportunity to oppose the demerger.

[151] Furthermore, pursuant to the Companies Act, the company must also notify in writing, at least one month prior to the due date mentioned in the public announcement, all those known creditors whose receivables have arisen prior to the registration of the demerger plan.

[152] As such, demerger proceedings do not result in premature payment of the debts of the demerging company. However, if a creditor opposes the demerger, the receivables of the creditor must be paid or a sufficient security placed to secure the payment of the creditor's receivables, and generally, such a solution must be reached within one month after the due date mentioned in the public announcement.

4. Approval of Demerger

[153] The demerger must be approved by both the demerging and the receiving company or companies within four months after the registration of the demerger plan. If the demerger is not approved without changes, the demerger is aborted.

[154] In the demerging company, a general meeting of shareholders must be convened to approve the demerger. The demerger is approved by the general meeting with a majority of two-thirds of votes cast and shares represented in the meeting (and, if there are different share classes, also two-thirds of shares of each share class represented in the meeting).

[155] In the receiving company/companies, the board of directors approves the demerger. However, if shareholders holding at least 5% of all shares in the company so demand, the demerger must be approved in a general meeting of shareholders. The shareholders need to be informed of the demerger in the same manner as a general meeting is convened.

5. Possible Redemption

[156] The shareholders (and possibly also any holders of warrants and other special rights) of the demerging company can, in the general meeting of shareholders that resolves upon the demerger, demand the redemption of their shares for cash. If the redemption cannot be agreed with the receiving company/companies, the dispute regarding the redemption (including the appropriate redemption price, which must equal the 'fair price' of the shares) will be settled in arbitration proceedings. Such arbitration proceedings should not, however, have any effect on the duration of the demerger process as the shareholders only have the right to the redemption price after the dispute is submitted into arbitration.

6. Execution of Demerger

[157] The demerger enters into force when the execution of the demerger has been registered with the Finnish Trade Register. The execution of the demerger must be applied with the Finnish Trade Register within six months from the resolutions approving the demerger. The execution of the demerger can only be applied for after the period of the public announcement has elapsed and either no creditor has opposed the demerger or the receivables of any opposing creditors have been settled or secured by a sufficient security. The execution of the demerger further requires a statement from the auditor confirming that the receiving company receives in the demerger full coverage for any amount added to its equity. When the demerger is registered, the assets and liabilities of the demerging company are transferred to the receiving company/companies without a liquidation process. As a condition for the execution of the demerger, foreign limited liability companies will have to adopt the demerger plan, relevant provisions of the Companies Act, such as right of redemption, as well as the rules regarding employee representation in European Companies (SE) and European Cooperative Societies (SCE), when applicable.

[158] With respect to a full demerger, the final financial accounts of the demerging company, up to the date of execution of the merger, must be prepared (and usually also audited) as soon as possible after the execution of the demerger. Thereafter, irrespective of the fact that the demerging company has already been dissolved by the execution of the demerger, the board of directors of the demerging company must convene a meeting of the shareholders of the demerging company, who must approve the final accounts. The final accounts must be filed for registration with the Finnish Trade Register within two months from the approval of the final accounts by the shareholders of the demerging company.

[159] The demerging company and the receiving company or companies remain jointly liable for the demerging company's existing liabilities, unless otherwise agreed in the demerger plan. In case liability for the existing debts has been limited in the demerger plan, the maximum liability of the company participating in the demerger will be the net value of the assets remaining or being transferred to such company. Furthermore, unless otherwise agreed between the creditors, a creditor can claim joint liability for such debts only after it has shown that the primary debtor is unable to pay the debt or to provide security for such payment. With regard to debts that are not mentioned in the demerger plan and which have arisen prior to the completion of the demerger, the receiving company/companies are liable for any such debts towards third-party creditors, should the demerging company fail to fulfil its obligations.

[160] With regard to the demerging company's agreements with third parties, as a general rule, the receiving company replaces the demerging company in the contractual relationship. However, agreements may include specific clauses that could be triggered by a demerger.

2.2 Overview of Securities Market Regulation

2.2.1 Regulatory Framework

General

[161] As in all EU Member States, EU directives and regulations are an integral part of the Finnish regulatory framework in addition to national securities legislation. The principal national statute governing the Finnish securities market is the Securities Market Act. In addition, the Finnish Financial Supervisory Authority (the 'FIN-FSA') and the Helsinki Stock Exchange (OMXH) have issued more detailed regulations pursuant to the Securities Market Act. The FIN-FSA monitors compliance with these regulations. The scope of the FIN-FSA's duties includes various supervisory tasks, including institutional, prudential, market and conduct of business supervision. The FIN-FSA also monitors insider trading.

[162] A new Finnish securities regulatory framework was introduced on 1 January 2013 in order to improve the clarity of securities market legislation, increase the competitiveness of securities markets and ease the administrative burden imposed on listed companies. Most significantly, the new regulatory framework changed the legislative structure by separating the former securities markets act into several new acts. However, the Securities Market Act still regulates the listing of securities, company and shareholder disclosure requirements and public tender offers, among other things. The rules regarding the operation of the stock exchange and some of the rules with regard to admission to listing and trading of listed securities are now regulated in the Act on Trading in Financial Instruments (1070/2017, as amended). The Securities Market Act no longer regulates insider trading, as the rules regarding insider trading are now included in the Market Abuse Regulation that came into effect on 3 July 2016.

[163] In addition to the statutes introduced above, the regulations and guidelines issued by the FIN-FSA and the Helsinki Takeover Code issued by the Finnish Securities Market Association (the 'Takeover Code') are an important part of the regulatory framework. The Takeover Code follows the 'comply or explain' principle, meaning a party not committed to complying with the code must provide an explanation for its non-compliance.

[164] Furthermore, listed companies should operate in compliance with the Corporate Governance Code issued by the Finnish Securities Market Association. The self-regulation aims to ensure that listed companies follow uniform and transparent operating principles and rules. Generally, the aim is to promote good corporate governance.

Listing of Securities

[165] According to the Act on Trading in Financial Instruments, a stock exchange can admit securities to be listed if it is likely that there would be sufficient demand and supply for a security, which further strengthens the presumption that the price formation for such security is reliable. Additional requirements are found in EU legislation, such as in Regulation (EU) 2017/1129 of the European Parliament and of the Council on the prospectus to be published when securities are offered to the public or admitted to trading on a regulated market ('Prospectus Regulation') as well as in national legislation, such as in the Securities Market Act. Furthermore, the rules of the Nasdaq Helsinki and First North Nordic rulebook, as well as unofficial translations, must be followed. These documents can be found online.

[166] The Prospectus Regulation specifies minimum disclosure requirements for companies applying for listing on the Nasdaq Helsinki or making a public offering of securities in Finland. The disclosure of information is necessary to enable investors to make informed investment decisions on the securities on offer. Finnish listed companies have a continuing obligation to publish financial information and to disclose any matters likely to have a material impact on the value of their securities.

Flagging Requirements

[167] A shareholder is required, without undue delay, to notify a Finnish listed company and the FIN-FSA when its voting interest in, or its percentage ownership of, the issued shares in such Finnish listed company reaches, exceeds or falls below 5%, 10%, 15%, 20%, 25%, 30%, 50%, 66.67% (2/3) and 90%, calculated in accordance with the Securities Market Act. The flagging obligation also applies to transactions by Finnish listed companies in respect of their treasury shares.

[168] Pursuant to the Securities Market Act, the flagging requirement also concerns financial instruments that entitle its holders to acquire such number of shares in a Finnish listed company, which reaches, exceeds or falls below the applicable threshold, or that would have a similar economic effect with such financial instruments. Also the combined amount of existing proportions of (i) holdings and voting rights pertaining to shares and (ii) financial instruments may trigger the flagging obligation.

[169] A shareholder is required to submit a flagging notification without undue delay and no later than on the next trading day after the shareholder knew or should have known of (i) the purchase or the sale, (ii) its possibility to use voting rights or (iii) the transaction due to which its voting rights or the percentage ownership of the issued shares in a Finnish listed company has changed or will change.

It is presumed that the shareholder knew about the transaction at the latest two trading days after such transaction took place.

2.2.2 Securities Market

Trading and Settlement on Nasdaq Helsinki

[170] Nasdaq Helsinki is a part of Nasdaq, which owns and maintains the Nasdaq stock market in New York as well as seven other European stock exchanges in Stockholm, Copenhagen, Riga, Tallinn, Vilnius, Reykjavik and Yerevan. The Nasdaq Nordic exchange consists of four local stock exchanges located in Helsinki, Stockholm, Copenhagen and Reykjavik. The four exchanges are separate legal entities in different jurisdictions but have been subject to harmonization within the major areas of regulation, including listing, cash equity trading and trading in derivatives. Companies are presented in segments based on market value and in sectors according to industry affiliation.

[171] Trading in the equities market on Nasdaq Helsinki (as well as for other Nordic and Baltic equities trading) takes place in the INET Nordic trading platform. Nasdaq Helsinki applies a two-day settlement cycle (T+2) with regard to all securities. The trading and clearing currency is the euro. The main trading phases of Nasdaq Helsinki are pre-trading, trading and post-trading. For shares, pre-trading at the prices established during the previous trading day begins at 9:00 a.m. and ends at 9:45 a.m. Regular trading with calls and continuous trading takes place from 10:00 a.m. to 6:25 p.m. Post-trading, during which only contract transactions for shares at the prices established during the trading day can be registered, takes place from 6:30 p.m. to 7:00 p.m. Trades are normally cleared on the second business day after the trade date (T+2) unless otherwise agreed by the parties.

[172] There are also alternative marketplaces for trading unlisted shares. Nasdaq First North Growth Market is an alternative stock exchange for smaller companies in the Nordic countries. Companies listed on First North are subject only to the rules of First North and not the requirements of a regulated market.

Finnish Book-Entry Securities System

[173] The use of the Finnish book-entry securities system is mandatory for companies whose shares are quoted on Nasdaq Helsinki. The Finnish book-entry securities system is centralized at Euroclear Finland, which offers national clearing, settlement and registration services for securities. Shares in a Finnish company may also be entered into a foreign book-entry system authorized in the EU region. Euroclear Finland maintains a central book-entry register for both equity and debt securities. In order to execute entries in the book-entry securities system, a security holder may either open a book-entry account with Euroclear Finland or an account operator or, with respect to a foreigner, foreign entity or trust, request that the securities be recorded on a book-entry account in the name of a bank, i.e., on a custodial nominee account. A custodial nominee account must contain information on the custodial account holder instead of the beneficial owner and indicate that the account is a custodial nominee account. Book-entry securities owned by one or more beneficial owners may be registered in a custodial nominee account. In addition, the securities owned by a foreigner, foreign entity or trust may be deposited in a book-entry account opened in the name of such foreigner, foreign entity or trust, but the holding may be registered in the name of a nominee in the company's register of shareholders. For shareholders who have not transferred their shares into book entries, a joint book-entry account is opened with Euroclear Finland with the issuer as the registered holder.

[174] Euroclear Finland and the account operators are required to observe strict confidentiality. Certain information (e.g., the name and address of each account holder) contained in the register of shareholders maintained by Euroclear Finland must be made available to the public by Euroclear Finland and the company, except in the case of custodial nominee registration. The FIN-FSA is also entitled to access certain information on the holdings of shares registered in a custodial nominee account upon request. The company has the same rights in respect of shares and instruments that entitle their holders to shares issued by the company.

Compensation Fund for Investors

[175] A compensation fund for investors was established in 1998. The fund does not compensate for any losses incurred by professional investors. The definition of a professional investor includes business enterprises and public entities, which are deemed to understand the securities markets and their associated risks. An investor may also provide notice in writing that, on the basis of his/her professional skills and experience in the securities markets, he/she is a professional investor. However, natural persons are presumed to be non-professional investors.

[176] Investment firms and credit institutions must participate in the compensation fund. The compensation fund safeguards payment of clear and indisputable claims when an investment company or a credit institution has been declared bankrupt is undergoing a restructuring process or is otherwise, for a reason other than temporary insolvency, not capable of paying claims within a determined period of time. For valid claims, the compensation fund will pay 90% of the investor's claim against each investment company or credit institution, up to a maximum of EUR20 000. The compensation fund does not provide compensation for losses due to decreases in stock value or bad investment decisions.

2.2.3 Public Takeovers

[177] The primary provisions governing public takeovers are (i) the Securities Market Act, (ii) regulations and guidelines issued by the FIN-FSA, and (iii) the Takeover Code. Takeovers may also fall under specific provisions of merger control under the applicable competition law, foreign direct investment law or industry-specific advance clearance depending on the target company (such as for banks and insurance companies). In addition, the articles of association of the target company may have an effect on the structure of the public tender offer. The articles of association might include certain provisions on majority requirements or provisions on compulsory acquisition of minority shares, which might have lower thresholds than those in the Securities Market Act.

Tender Offers

Initial Announcement, Notifications, and Financing

[178] As soon as the board of directors (or another competent corporate body) of the bidder has decided to launch a tender offer, such decision must be disclosed in a public announcement by submitting a notice of the tender offer to the target company, the FIN-FSA and Nasdaq Helsinki. The offer must also be notified to the representatives of the employees in both the target company and the bidder.

[179] The rules of Nasdaq Helsinki require a listed company to notify Nasdaq Helsinki of a contemplated tender offer where the company is making internal preparations regarding a tender offer for securities of another listed company if it deems that there are reasonable grounds to assume that such preparations will result in the launching of such tender offer. Nasdaq Helsinki must also be notified if a listed company has become aware that a third party is planning to launch a tender offer for its shares. Information supplied to Nasdaq Helsinki is not made public and the exchange uses the information mainly for its trading surveillance activities.

[180] Prior to the announcement of a tender offer, the Securities Market Act requires the bidder to secure financing for the tender offer. In respect of any cash consideration, the bidder must have sufficient cash reserves or, alternatively, it must have secured binding financing for the offer. The financing arrangements may, however, be subject to conditions precedent in accordance with normal market practice (e.g., no material adverse change in market conditions or the target company's business).

Due Diligence in Public Takeovers

[181] Due to extensive disclosure obligations set forth in the Securities Market Act for listed companies, Finnish companies are responsible for disclosing a wide range of information to the market. This includes information which might materially affect the value of a security. Listed companies must publish annual financial statements and annual reviews, corporate governance statements, audit reports, financial statement releases, as well as interim reports for the first six months of each financial period. In practice, listed companies also publish interim reports for the first three and nine months of each financial period.

[182] In addition to the information disclosed directly by listed companies, a vast array of information about listed companies, such as trade register extracts and articles of association, are also publicly available for a nominal fee from the Finnish Patent and Registration Office.

[183] For a listed company to allow a due diligence review, there must be a special reason present. Usually, such reason manifests itself by being in the best interest of the target company's shareholders. Although most takeover bid situations call for a due diligence review, the scope and schedule of such review must be separately considered by the board of directors. Individual aspects relating to the situation as well as competition law considerations and the likelihood of the bid being completed must be weighed in.

[184] In order for the board of directors of a target company to be able to make a well-founded assessment on a public takeover bid, they should acquire sufficient and appropriate information about the securities possibly offered as consideration and, for this purpose, conduct a due diligence review regarding the bidder, if necessary.

Tender Offer Document and Timing

[185] The bidder must publish a tender offer document (prospectus) prior to the commencement of a tender offer. In a voluntary tender offer, there is no statutory time limit for the commencement of the tender offer after the announcement of the bidder's decision to launch such offer. However, the FIN-FSA recommends that the bidder should not delay the commencement of the tender offer without cause. In voluntary all-cash tender offers, the FIN-FSA views one month as a reasonable time to commence the tender offer. The tender offer document must contain substantial and adequate information for the evaluation of the fairness of the tender offer.

[186] Before publishing and distributing the tender offer document to the public, the bidder must file the document with the FIN-FSA for approval. The tender offer document cannot be filed with the FIN-FSA before the announcement of the launch of the tender offer by the bidder. The FIN-FSA must decide within five business days (or ten or twenty business days in case the offer price is paid in the form of securities of the bidder) after the filing (excluding the filing date) whether or not the tender offer document is to be made public. After obtaining FIN-FSA approval, the bidder may publish the tender offer document by filing the document with the target company and with Nasdaq Helsinki. The target company must notify the offer to the representative of its employees. The tender offer period may commence no earlier than the date of approval by the FIN-FSA of the tender offer document.

[187] The bidder is required to amend or supplement the tender offer document without undue delay prior to the expiry of the offer period if it contains a material misrepresentation or omission. Such amendment or supplement must be submitted for approval to the FIN-FSA before it can be published, and, in connection with the approval, the FIN-FSA may require the bidder to extend the offer period by up to ten business days.

Buyer Exclusivity and Break Fees

[188] The bidder and the target company typically enter into a combination agreement on the execution of the takeover process, although such agreement is not required by law or regulations. The target company may commit to a 'buyer exclusivity', in which the board refrains from actively seeking competing bids. In case of possible superior competing offers, the boards always retain the right to end the exclusivity with the first bidder. The target company may also commit to a break fee (usually limited to cost reimbursement). However, possible contractual arrangements affecting the takeover process must be in line with the obligations of the board of directors set forth in the Companies Act, the Securities Market Act and the

Takeover Code. As such, these arrangements must always be in the best interest of the target company's shareholders.

Offer Period

[189] The offer period for the tender offer must be at least three weeks and may not exceed ten weeks. In specific circumstances (such as pending regulatory approvals), the offer period may exceed ten weeks, provided that the business of the target company is not hindered for an unreasonable period of time. If the target company convenes a general meeting of shareholders to assess the tender offer, the FIN-FSA may, at the request of the target company, require the bidder to extend the offer period until such general meeting has been held. The FIN-FSA may issue such an order without giving the bidder a hearing in the matter. However, if the FIN-FSA issues such an order, the bidder may withdraw its tender offer within five business days from the receipt of such order.

Conditional Tender Offers and Amendment of Terms and Conditions

[190] The bidder may make a voluntary tender offer subject to closing conditions. The bidder may also reserve the right to waive such closing conditions. Even a conditional tender offer is binding upon the bidder, and the bidder may withdraw its offer only if permitted by the Securities Market Act, e.g., if a competing tender offer is made or if the closing conditions are not fulfilled.

Competing Tender Offer

[191] If a competing tender offer is made, the first bidder may extend the offer period to match that of the competing offer and/or amend the terms and conditions of its own offer. The first bidder may also decide to withdraw its offer. Moreover, if a competing tender offer is launched, the security holders may withdraw their acceptance of the first tender offer during the offer period of the first tender offer even if the first tender offer has been declared unconditional but before the sale has been done. A tender offer becomes unconditional when the closing conditions of the tender offer are fulfilled.

[192] Furthermore, if a competing tender offer is launched, the first bidder is required to supplement its tender offer document with information concerning the competing offer. The FIN-FSA has stated that it may require the first bidder to extend the offer period of its tender offer in such a manner that the offer period is open for a minimum of ten business days from the publishing of the supplement to the first bidder's tender offer document. Finally, it should be noted that the provisions of the Securities Market Act on competing offers will apply only if a competing offer is officially made – if a third party merely announces that it is contemplating making a competing offer, such provisions will not apply.

Mandatory Tender Offer Obligation

[193] The Securities Market Act provides that a shareholder who shall come to hold shares representing more than 30% of the total voting rights represented by a listed company's shares must offer to purchase in cash the remaining shares of the company and any share derivatives issued by the company (redemption obligation). The redemption obligation will not, however, be triggered if there is another shareholder who has a larger shareholding in the target company. In such case, the redemption obligation will be triggered only after the shareholding exceeds the shareholding of such larger shareholder. A similar redemption obligation also exists when the threshold of 50% has been exceeded.

[194] The bidder is not required to launch a mandatory tender offer if the voting rights threshold has been exceeded pursuant to a public tender offer provided that the tender offer has been made for all the shares and share derivatives issued by the target company or by acquiring securities during the offer period of such tender offer.

[195] If a voting rights threshold is exceeded solely due to measures taken by the target company or by another shareholder, the redemption obligation will not arise before such shareholder acquires or subscribes to more shares of the target company or otherwise raises his holding of voting rights in the target company.

[196] There is no redemption obligation if exceeding the applicable voting rights threshold is due to the shareholders acting in concert when making a voluntary tender offer and when such action is limited only to such offer. Also, there will be no redemption obligation if the party under such obligation, or another party who is acting in concert with such party, gives up its voting rights in excess of the applicable threshold. This has to be done within one month of exceeding the threshold either by transferring the shareholding in the target company or by otherwise decreasing the voting rights in the target company. The shareholder must immediately announce its intention to decrease its shareholding below the applicable threshold. In addition, such shareholder may not exercise any voting rights in respect of its shareholding in the target company before its shareholding has decreased below the applicable threshold.

[197] The Securities Market Act contains detailed provisions on how a shareholder's holding in a listed company is calculated for the purposes of the redemption obligation. In addition to directly held shares, shares held by subsidiaries and other entities controlled by the shareholder are also taken into account as well as shares held together with a third party and shares held by persons who act in concert with the shareholder in question. Therefore, it is not possible to circumvent the obligation to make a mandatory tender offer through indirect shareholdings.

Disclosure and Timing of Mandatory Tender Offer

[198] When a redemption obligation is triggered, the shareholder in question must immediately disclose such obligation with a public announcement. In addition, the triggering of the obligation must be notified to the target company, the FIN-FSA and Nasdaq Helsinki. The triggering of the obligation must also be notified to the representatives of the employees in both the target company and the shareholder.

[199] The shareholder in question must publish the terms and conditions of the mandatory tender offer within one month from the triggering of the redemption obligation. The offer period must, in turn, commence within one month from the publication of the terms and conditions.

Pricing

Pricing Requirements

[200] Generally, the Securities Market Act provides that any person making a tender offer for publicly traded shares and/or share derivatives may not place the holders of such securities in an unequal position.

[201] In a voluntary tender offer, the offer price may be freely paid in cash, in securities or in a combination thereof. However, the bidder must offer a cash consideration at least as an alternative, if: (i) an exchange offer is made for all the shares and share derivatives of the target company and shares offered as consideration are not subject to public trading in any EEA country nor will such shares be listed in connection with the offer, or (ii) the bidder has, during the period commencing six months before the launch of the tender offer and ending at the expiry thereof, purchased, with cash, securities of the target company entitling it to at least 5% of the voting rights in the target company.

[202] The Securities Market Act requires that the offer price for the shares being purchased in connection with a mandatory tender offer must be a 'fair price'. In a mandatory tender offer, securities or combination of cash and securities can only be offered as an alternative to all-cash consideration.

[203] The minimum offer price in: (i) a voluntary tender offer for all shares and share derivatives of the target company, and (ii) a mandatory tender offer is the highest price paid by the bidder during the six months preceding the announcement of the voluntary tender offer or the triggering of the obligation to launch a mandatory tender offer, as applicable. In a voluntary tender offer, if the bidder has not purchased any shares of the target company during the six-month period, the bidder may freely set the offer price for all shares and share derivatives of the target company. In a mandatory tender offer, if the bidder has not purchased any shares of the target company during the six-month period, the minimum offer price is the volume-weighted average market price for the securities during the three-month period preceding the triggering of the obligation to make a mandatory tender offer. If special reasons exist, such as purchases by the bidder at a higher price than the offer price during the twelve months preceding the tender offer, the offer price may deviate from the above-mentioned prices.

[204] The Securities Market Act does not regulate the pricing of voluntary tender offers which are not made for all shares and share derivatives in the target company. However, if the obligation to launch a mandatory tender offer arises as a result of such voluntary tender offer, the above-mentioned provisions on pricing of mandatory tender offers would naturally need to be observed.

Top-up and Compensation Obligation

[205] If, after the announcement of the tender offer but before the end of the offer period, the bidder purchases equity securities of the target company outside the tender offer at a price which is higher than the offer price or otherwise on better terms, the bidder is required to amend the terms and conditions and price of the tender offer to match the better terms and higher price paid to the shareholders of the target company who tendered their securities in the tender offer (top-up obligation).

[206] Further, the bidder is required to pay to the target company's shareholders the difference between the offered price and any compensation paid by the bidder for such securities during a nine-month period after the expiration of the tender offer (compensation obligation). However, the bidder is not required to pay the difference between the offered price and any compensation received by the bidder for the sale of such securities afterwards.

Exemptions Granted by the FIN-FSA

[207] The Securities Market Act gives the FIN-FSA the right to grant exemptions from the obligations related to tender offers, including the obligation to make a mandatory tender offer. The FIN-FSA considers such exemptions on a case-by-case basis. The FIN-FSA has indicated that it may be willing to grant exemptions from the obligation to make a mandatory tender offer if certain preconditions are met, for example, when the mandatory offer threshold is exceeded in connection with a transaction where the ultimate purpose of such transaction is not obtaining control or significant influence in the target company.

Role of the Target Company in Tender Offers

Finnish Corporate Law Principles

[208] Certain Finnish corporate law principles must be taken into account when the target company's board of directors is considering possible actions in connection with a proposed public tender offer or an announcement concerning a public tender offer. Such principles have been set out in the Companies Act and Takeover Code.

Duties of the Board in Tender Offer Situations

[209] To fulfil its obligations, the board of directors of the target company should take an active role in connection with a potential takeover. The Securities Market Act and the Takeover Code set forth several duties for the board of directors, which include managing the tender offer process in a controlled manner so as to provide the board of directors with an opportunity to diligently assess the tender offer and its fairness.

Considering a Tender Offer Proposal

[210] If the board of directors is contacted with a tender offer proposal and considers such contact to be of a serious and credible nature and the offered price (including any premium) is at least potentially attractive, the board of directors should evaluate what measures may be required to secure the interests of the shareholders of the target company. This requires careful evaluation of the tender offer itself as well as other alternatives available.

Possible Cooperation with the Bidder

[211] If the board of directors concludes in its evaluation that the proposed tender offer appears to be the most beneficial alternative available for the shareholders, the board of directors should generally, in accordance with its fiduciary duty, strive to achieve the highest possible price for the securities of the target company, and it should examine whether the bidder has the necessary prerequisites to complete the tender offer. To secure the highest possible price, the board of directors should, as a general rule, act in such a manner that all serious competing bidders have an equal opportunity to launch a tender offer for the securities of the target company.

Opposing the Tender Offer

[212] The board of directors may in its evaluation conclude that the (proposed) tender offer is not in the best interest of the shareholders. In such case, the board of directors may be satisfied in only stating this view in its statement, or it may also seek to take defensive action. Based on the general principles of the Companies Act, however, it has been concluded in Finnish legal commentary that the board of directors may undertake defensive measures that have the purpose of preventing the completion of a tender offer only in very exceptional cases. Pursuant to the Takeover Code, if the board of directors, after having received information on a contemplated tender offer, intends to oppose or take defensive measures against the tender offer, it should typically convene a general meeting of shareholders to consider the planned defensive measures. Such measures may include, among others, the sale of core assets of the target company or transactions that deviate from the ordinary course of business of the target company or are otherwise not in accordance with normal market practice.

Statement Regarding the Tender Offer

[213] The board of directors of the target company must issue a statement regarding the tender offer. The board of directors must provide its statement to the best of its abilities, and such statement must include an assessment of the tender offer from the viewpoint of the target company and its shareholders. In addition, the statement must include an assessment of the strategic plans of the bidder as presented in the tender offer document and their likely effects on the operations of the target company and employment in the target company.

[214] In its statement, the board of directors must take a view on the tender offer and provide guidance to the shareholders of the target company. However, the statement does not necessarily need to include a definitive recommendation to the shareholders to approve or reject the tender offer. If no such recommendation is included in the statement, the board of directors should explain the reasons for not being able to recommend either the approval or rejection of the tender offer.

[215] If the board of directors is not able to evaluate the merits of the tender offer, it must state this in its statement and provide grounds for this view. Also, if the board of directors has not made a unanimous decision regarding the contents of the statement, this must be set forth in the statement.

[216] The statement of the board of directors must be published as soon as possible after the tender offer document has been delivered to the target company and, in any event, no later than five business days prior to the expiration of the tender offer period.

[217] There is no obligation for the board of directors to use external experts in preparing its statement. However, in many cases, to fulfil its duty of care, the board of directors obtains a fairness opinion from a reputable investment bank. Also, due to the rather complex and technical nature of the Finnish takeover rules, it is customary for the board of directors of a target company to seek legal advice in connection with a tender offer.

Competing Tender Offers

[218] If the board of directors of the target company receives a contact of a serious nature from a competing bidder, the board of directors should assess the situation, acquire sufficient and appropriate information on the competing proposal and compare the proposal with the first (proposed) tender offer. To secure the highest possible consideration for the securities of the target company, the board of directors should, as a general rule, act in such a manner that all serious competing bidders have equal opportunity to launch a tender offer for the securities of the target company.

[219] According to the Securities Market Act, if a competing tender offer is made where the board of directors has already made public its statement on the initial tender offer, the board of directors should supplement its statement on the initial tender offer as soon as possible after the competing tender offer has been announced. In such supplemental statement, the board of directors should impartially compare the initial tender offer with the competing tender offer and express its opinion on the new competing tender offer. The statement should be supplemented no later than five business days prior to the expiration of the initial tender offer period.

Possible Post-Takeover Measures

Disclosure Obligations

[220] After the expiry of the offer period, the bidder must make public the result of the tender offer, and disclose its resolution to initiate squeeze-out proceedings, if applicable. The target company must, through its own press release, also make public the notification given by the bidder regarding the result of the tender offer. Furthermore, the target company has a continuous duty to disclose all information regarding the company that is likely to have a material effect on the value of the securities of the company.

[221] The target company must also be notified without delay when the bidder's shareholdings either: (i) increase to more than 90% of all shares and voting rights, or (ii) decrease to 90% or less of all shares and voting rights. The Companies Act provides that the company receiving such notification must, without undue delay, notify this to the Finnish Trade Register.

[222] Failure to deliver the above notifications to the target company does not have any effect on the redemption right (or obligation) as such, but such failure may result in an obligation to compensate for any damage resulting from the failure to receive notification.

Minority Squeeze-Out

[223] Chapter 18 of the Companies Act provides that a shareholder holding more than 90% of all shares and voting rights of a company has the right to redeem (or squeeze-out) the remaining shares of the company from the minority shareholders at a 'fair price'. The 90% shareholder also has an obligation to redeem the shares of any minority-shareholder if such minority-shareholder demands the redemption of its shares.

[224] The redemption price (or squeeze-out price) for shares held by minority shareholders is, as a general rule, the 'fair price' at the time preceding the initiation of arbitration proceedings aimed at resolving the fair price of the shares, and generally refers to the market price of the shares at such time. However, when the redemption right (or obligation) arises after a mandatory tender offer or a voluntary tender offer that was accepted by shareholders representing more than 90% of the shares that were subject to the tender offer, the redemption price is generally determined by the price offered in the preceding tender offer or mandatory tender offer, unless special reasons are deemed to exist for a deviation from such price.

[225] Irrespective of the above general rule, certain conditions may result in the price offered in the preceding tender offer or mandatory tender offer being disregarded in determining the 'fair price'. For example, if a relatively long time has passed after the tender offer or mandatory tender offer, or if only a small number of shareholders to whom the offer was directed accepted the preceding tender offer, this could indicate that the price offered might not reflect the 'fair price' for the shares.

Delisting

[226] In accordance with the Nasdaq Helsinki rules, the exchange may, upon application by a listed company, terminate trading in the listed company's securities. Such delisting may not result in any significant damage to investors or to the orderly operation of the securities markets. In a takeover situation, such delisting of shares requires a full ownership of the listed company by the acquirer.

2.3 Regulated Industries

2.3.1 Financial Sector

[227] The FIN-FSA is the principal authority responsible for supervising the financial markets and regulatory compliance in Finland. The FIN-FSA is also responsible for granting licenses relating to various operations in the financial sector in Finland.

[228] Operating as a credit institution in Finland requires a license, which is granted by the European Central Bank upon application made to the FIN-FSA. The FIN-FSA also grants licenses to the following entities: (i) life, non-life and reinsurance companies; (ii) payment institutions and electronic money institutions; (iii) investment firms; (iv) fund management companies and custodians and (v) managers of alternative investment funds. In addition to the above-mentioned activities subject to licensing/authorization from the FIN-FSA, the following activities are subject to registration with the FIN-FSA: (i) mortgage credit intermediaries; (ii) intermediation of loan-based crowdfunding; (iii) acting as a bondholders' representative; (iv) sale of insurance on behalf of an insurance company; (v) acting as an insurance broker; and (vi) virtual currency providers. Peer loan intermediaries are required to register with the Finnish Regional State Administrative Agency and fundraising requires a license issued by the Police forces and the National Police Board.

[229] Licenses for securities and derivatives exchanges as well as central securities depositories are granted by the Ministry of Finance. The Council of State grants licenses for employment pension insurance companies and the Ministry of Social Affairs and Health for unemployment funds.

[230] The Credit Institutions Act (610/2014, as amended) is the principal act regulating the banking sector in Finland. The act is compatible with the Third Basel Accord and applies to all banking (where repayable funds are accepted from the public and credit or other financing is offered at the relevant credit institution's own account) and deposit-taking activities. It also sets forth the principles of supervision for such credit operations. In addition to the Credit Institutions Act, there are a number of other specific laws which relate to particular corporate forms of banking, such as the Act on Commercial Banks and Other Credit Institutions in the Form of a Limited Company (1501/2001, as amended), the Savings Bank Act (1502/2001, as amended) and the Act on Cooperative Banks and Other Credit Institutions in the Form of a Cooperative (423/2013, as amended).

[231] The operations and supervision of both domestic and foreign investment firms are regulated in the Act on Investment Services (747/2012, as amended). The Act on Payment Institutions (297/2010, as amended) and the Act on Payment Services (290/2010, as amended) regulate the provision of payment services in Finland.

[232] In addition, all companies operating in the financial sector are required to comply with the Act on Prevention of Money Laundering (444/2017, as amended). The law prohibits banks and financial institutions from engaging in money laundering activities and, among other things, requires such institutions to report to the police transactions suspected of being money laundering. The Finnish anti-money laundering regulation applies to both national and cross-border activities.

[233] In addition to the applicable laws, detailed requirements and provisions relating to the operations of licensed entities are set out in government decrees and rules and regulations of the FIN-FSA. Rules and regulations of the FIN-FSA include both legally binding regulations and recommended guidelines.

Prerequisites for a License

[234] In general, a license is granted only when the entity applying for a license meets the necessary regulatory requirements. The requirements include the following criteria: (i) that the company is managed in a professional manner and according to sound and prudent business principles; (ii) that the company has sound internal governance measures and adequate financial resources; (iii) that the company's business operations are planned, managed, organized and controlled according to high professional and ethical standards; and (iv) the organization has its headquarters in Finland.

[235] Detailed conditions governing the licenses for credit institutions, investment firms, fund management companies, payment institutions and custodians are set out in the Credit Institutions Act, the Act on Investment Firms, the Act on Payment Institutions and the Mutual Funds Act (213/2019, as amended) as well as applicable government decrees and FIN-FSA rules, regulations and guidelines.

Application for License

[236] The application for an operating license must be submitted to the FIN-FSA, with supporting documents attached. Pre-filing meetings and discussions are not required by law but are strongly recommended by the FIN-FSA. Once the application has been filed, in respect of a banking license, the FIN-FSA must provide the European Central Bank with its proposed decision within four months of receipt of the relevant application (or, if the application is incomplete, within four months of receipt of any outstanding documents and materials). For investment firms, fund management companies and custodians, the FIN-FSA must announce its decision within six months of receipt of the application (or, if the application is incomplete, within six months of receipt by the FIN-FSA of a duly completed application).

[237] A final decision on a license application must always be issued to credit institutions, investment firms, fund management companies and custodians within twelve months from receipt of the application. For insurance companies, the time limit is six months. Payment institutions must be issued a decision within three months from receipt of the relevant license application, provided that the application includes all the required information.

Notification of Acquisition of Ownership

[238] Acquisition of significant ownership in certain FIN-FSA supervised entities is subject to a notification obligation. For example, any person or entity who contemplates acquiring direct or indirect ownership of more than 10% of the voting rights in a credit institution, payment institution or fund management company must submit a prior written notification to the FIN-FSA. If the ownership is further increased to 20%, 30% or 50%, a new notification must be submitted prior to completion of the acquisition.

[239] In connection with the notification regarding the acquisition referred to above, the acquirer must also provide the FIN-FSA with a so-called fit and proper notification regarding the reliability and eligibility of the shareholders. The evaluation is the same as is conducted concerning the management of the supervised entity. In evaluating the reliability and eligibility of the shareholders, the FIN-FSA will assess, on the basis of the information received, the reliability, reputation, experience and eligibility of shareholder, and whether it can be ascertained that the organization will be managed in a professional manner and according to sound and prudent business principles.

Banking Operations by Foreign Entities

[240] A foreign entity which has been granted a banking license in its home country in the EEA may engage in credit institution activities (Fi: *luottolaitostoiminta*) covered by the license issued by the relevant supervisory authority in its home country in Finland either by establishing a branch office in Finland or by providing cross-border services without establishing a physical presence in the country.

[241] In case a branch office is planned to be established in Finland by an entity engaging in credit institution activities, establishing such branch office is subject to the FIN-FSA receiving a prior notification to this effect from the home country supervisory authority if the home country is a Member State of the EEA. In case the relevant entity is licensed by a non-EEA country, the FIN-FSA must first grant a license before such institution may operate as a credit institution in Finland, subject to limited exceptions relating to the provision of investment services. With respect to granting a license for a local branch of a credit institution licensed outside the EEA, the FIN-FSA will request an opinion from the Bank of Finland and the Deposit Guarantee Fund if the credit institution accepts deposits as well as a separate opinion from the Investor Compensation Fund if the credit institution provides investment services.

[242] The establishment of a Finnish branch office of a credit institution licensed in a non-EEA country is subject to, among other things, the following: (i) the activities of the credit institution do not materially differ from those permitted for Finnish credit institutions; (ii) the legislation applicable to the credit institution in its home country adheres to internationally accepted financial supervision standards and recommendations concerning the prevention of criminal abuse of the financial system; (iii) the branch office may pursuant to its home country legislation and license accept deposits from the public and the protection afforded to parties making deposits under such home country legislation does not materially differ from similar Finnish legislation; (iv) the credit institution's solvency, liquidity, internal compliance and supervision, risk management systems and fit and reliability of its management do not materially differ from the requirements of the Credit Institutions Act; and (v) the credit institution is subject to adequate supervision in its home country.

[243] In case no branch office is established, a credit institution licensed in an EEA country may provide cross-border services by notifying the relevant authorities. Such operations are subject to supervision by their home country's supervisory authority. Services can be offered when the FIN-FSA has received a notification of the provision of services from the supervisory authority of the home country. The notification shall contain a description of the types of services that the foreign institution intends to offer in Finland.

Insurance Companies

[244] In Finland, the conduct of insurance business is subject to obtaining a license from the FIN-FSA, which grants licenses for domestic life, non-life and reinsurance companies as well as insurance companies from outside the EEA. Non-domestic insurance companies domiciled within the EEA may generally conduct insurance business in Finland subject to notification from their home country supervisor. The Council of State grants licenses for employment pension insurance companies. The insurance sector is supervised by the FIN-FSA, which is the national authority for the supervision of Finland's financial and insurance sectors. The objective of the FIN-FSA is to ensure financial stability and balanced operations of regulated insurance companies and to safeguard the interests of the insured.

[245] Insurance legislation in Finland contains separate laws on domestic insurance companies, foreign insurance companies, authorized pension insurance companies, insurance associations, insurance brokers and insurance contracts and is based mostly on EU directives and, therefore, to a large extent harmonized with EU legislation. The main legislation in the insurance sector includes the Act on Insurance Companies (521/2008, as amended), the Act on the Supervision of Financial and Insurance Conglomerates (699/2004, as amended), the Act on Foreign Insurance Companies (398/1995, as amended), the Employee Pensions Act (395/2006, as amended), the Employment Accidents Act (459/2015, as amended) and the Insurance Contracts Act (543/1994, as amended).

[246] In Finland, social security is arranged on the basis of statutory insurance. The main insurance-based social security is the earnings-related pension. The earnings-related pensions in the private sector are handled by authorized pension insurance companies, pension funds, pension foundations, the Seafarer's Pensions Fund and the Farmer's Social Insurance Institution. The state employees' earnings-related pension as well as the earnings-related pension of municipal sector employees is handled by KEVA. In addition to the FIN-FSA, there are also some other authorities and organizations that supervise the insurance sector. For example, the Finnish Centre for Pensions supervises the fulfilment of employer insurance obligations to employees, whereas the Workers' Compensation Center (Fi: *Tapaturmavakuutuskeskus*) and the Finnish Occupational Safety and Health Administration (Fi: *Työsuojelu*) supervise employer obligations to employees in matters of accident insurance covering workplace accidents and occupational diseases. In addition, the Centres for Economic Development, Transport and the Environment ensure that companies whose activities may cause an environmental hazard to have proper insurance for any potential environmental damage for which they may be liable.

2.3.2 Energy Market – Electricity and Natural Gas Markets

[247] The main legislation in the energy market sector includes the Electricity Market Act (588/2013, as amended) and the Natural Gas Market Act (587/2017, as amended). The Energy Authority (Fi: *Energiavirasto*) (the EMA) is the national regulatory authority for electricity and natural gas markets as well as, among other things, the implementation of national and EU policies regarding renewable energy and maintenance of the Finnish renewable energy tariff system. The principal tasks of the EMA include regulating the pricing and the terms of transmission, distribution and other network services in both the electricity and the natural gas markets. The regulatory actions relating to the transmission and distribution system operators take place mainly on an *ex ante* basis. In addition, the EMA supervises the generation and supply sectors. This supervision of markets, including supply prices, is mainly *ex post* supervision. The EMA also promotes efficient competition in both the electricity and the natural gas trade, e.g., by intervening with respect to terms and prices of network services that are considered to restrict competition. Both electricity and natural gas network operations are subject to a license. The EMA grants network licenses to organizations and utilities engaged in network operation and building permits to companies constructing power lines carrying voltages of 110 kilovolts (kV) or more.

Electricity Market

[248] The opening of the Finnish electricity market commenced in 1995 and the development of that market has continued gradually. Under current legislation, all end-users of electricity may freely choose their electricity suppliers and the sale of electricity does not require a license. Only the power network operations, which have been preserved as a natural monopoly, call for an electricity network license from the EMA, provided, however, that no license is required where the electricity network is only applied for electricity delivery within a single property or comparable group of properties.

[249] There are three types of electricity network licenses: (i) an electricity network license for network operators operating distribution networks or high voltage distribution networks; (ii) an electricity network license for distribution network operators with responsibility for ensuring distribution to a specific geographic region specified in the license; and (iii) an electricity network license for the Finnish transmission network operator Fingrid Oyj. In special cases where the electricity network of the operator is of minor significance within the local electricity transmission, the EMA may allow a network operator to operate without a license. A license may be granted to an entity, municipal body or a state body and is in force until further notice, or, on special grounds, for a specified period. A license may be granted if the applicant has the technical, economic and organizational capabilities needed for conducting the proposed electricity network operations. Electricity network licenses are not transferable.

[250] Moreover, pursuant to the Electricity Market Act, the construction of a power line with a nominal voltage of 110 kV or more requires a permit from the EMA. In case of a domestic high voltage power line, the license is obtained from the EMA and, in the case of a cross-border power line, from the Ministry of Economic Affairs and Employment of Finland. No license is required for the construction of an internal power line inside an individual property or a comparable group of properties.

Natural Gas Market

[251] The natural gas markets in Finland have traditionally been very different from the natural gas markets in most of the other EU Member States. In continental Europe, the natural gas pipeline network covers the entire area and the supply of natural gas to private households and other small consumers plays an important role. The Finnish natural gas network has, however, been opened up to competition as of 1 January 2020 and currently, natural gas is available in approximately forty different localities through the network of natural gas pipelines.

[252] In the past, Finland has been dependent on Russian natural gas imports and received all of its natural gas supplies through a single pipeline from Russia. In the aftermath of the Russian invasion of Ukraine, Russia cut its natural gas supply to Finland. Finnish natural gas users now purchase natural gas from the Baltics and LNG from the Klaipeda natural gas terminal by way of the Balticconnector, a gas pipeline connecting the gas networks of Finland and Estonia which was opened at the end of 2019 to help secure the supply of natural gas in the region. As of 1 January 2020, Gasgrid Finland Oy has been granted system responsibility for the entire Finnish natural gas transmission network. After the opening of the Finnish gas market, import and wholesale of natural gas have been made possible for all operators that have registered as market participants.

[253] The two main permits needed by natural gas transmission network operators in Finland are the network license and project permission for the construction of a cross-border pipeline. The network license is the basic permit required to operate a pipeline, and the project permit concerns the building of cross-border pipelines. The natural gas network license is granted by the EMA until further notice or, under particular circumstances, for a specified period of time. The license can be granted to a municipal plant or to a corporation. In an individual case, the EMA may exempt the network operator from the license requirement for a specified period of time or until further notice if the network operator's natural gas network is of minor significance in terms of total natural gas transmission. Gasgrid Finland Oy has been granted a natural gas network license for the operation of the natural gas transmission network in Finland. The Ministry of Economic Affairs and Employment of Finland grants licenses for the construction of cross-border pipelines. Network licenses for operating natural gas networks cannot be transferred, whereas permits for constructing cross-border pipelines may only be transferred with the explicit consent of the Ministry of Economic Affairs and Employment of Finland.

Emissions Trading

[254] In January 2005, the EU's Emission Trading Scheme (ETS) commenced operation based on Directive 2003/87/EC of the European Parliament and of the Council of 13 October 2003 establishing a scheme for greenhouse gas emission allowance trading within the Community. In Finland, Directive 2003/87/EC was transposed into national law in August 2004 by the Emissions Trading Act (683/2004, as amended), which was subsequently repealed by the Finnish Emissions Trading Act (311/2011, as amended). Allowances traded in the EU's ETS are held in accounts in electronic registries set up by the EU Member States, which are overseen by a central administrator at the EU level. In Finland, the EMA acts as the National Emissions Trading Authority. The EMA grants the emissions permits that give installations the right to emit carbon dioxide (CO2) into the atmosphere, supervises the monitoring and reporting of emissions data and maintains the Emissions Trading Registry of Finland. The Finnish Transport and Communications Agency (Traficom) is responsible for emissions trading relating to air traffic in Finland.

[255] At the EU level, Directive (EU) 2018/410 of the European Parliament and of the Council of 14 March 2018 amending Directive 2003/87/EC was adopted in March 2018 as part of the EU's climate change package and will apply for Phase IV of the ETS, i.e., from 2021 to 2030. The purpose of the Directive is to improve and extend the greenhouse gas emission allowance trading scheme. The changes introduced by Directive (EU) 2018/410 have been implemented as amendments to the Finnish Emissions Trading Act.

[256] According to Finnish law, the enforcement of said Directive in the Åland Islands belongs to the legislative power of the province. The Emissions Trading Act is applied with minor exemptions in the Åland Islands as well. The provincial government makes a proposition for the European Commission about the allocation of allowances and grants the emissions permits to installations situated in the Åland Islands. The EMA is, however, in charge of registering the permits and other issues related to the Emissions Trading Registry.

2.3.3 Communications Market

Legislation and Regulatory Authorities

[257] The key legislation in the communications market sector consists of various acts and legislation based on EU directives. The main act in the sector is the Electronic Communication Services Act (917/2014, as amended). Another important act related to the communications market sector is the Finnish Broadcasting Company Act (1380/1993, as amended).

[258] The Ministry of Transport and Communications is responsible for general telecommunications supervision and development in Finland. The Finnish Transport and Communications Agency (Traficom) operates under the Ministry of Transport and Communications. The National Cyber Security Centre (NCSC-FI), operating under Traficom, supervises compliance of the Electronic Communication Services Act and regulations issued under it. The Ministry of Transport and Communications and the above-mentioned authorities work in cooperation with the competition and consumer authorities.

Communications Market Act

[259] The objective of the Electronic Communication Services Act is to promote the provision and use of electronic communications services and to ensure that communications networks and communications services are available under reasonable terms to everyone throughout the country. The aim is also to secure efficient and interference-free use of radio frequencies, to promote competition and to ensure that the communications networks and services are technologically advanced, of high-quality, reliable, safe, and inexpensive. The Electronic Communication Services Act also aims to safeguard the confidentiality of electronic communication and protection of privacy.

License and Notification

[260] The Electronic Communication Services Act makes a distinction between network services and communications services. The provision of a network service that uses radio frequencies requires a license. Other public telecommunications operations only require a written notification. The network service operations are subject to a license due to the limited amount of available radio frequencies.

[261] Usually, a license is granted by the Council of State for a fixed period of up to twenty years. Once frequencies that are technically appropriate for efficient frequency use become available, the Council of State announces a license available for application. The requirements for the granting of a license are: (i) the applicant must have sufficient economic resources to meet the network operator obligations; (ii) the licensing authority has no justifiable reason to suspect that the applicant will violate the communications legislation; and (iii) the licensing authority has no significantly weighty reason to suspect that granting of the license would materially endanger the national security. If a license cannot be granted to all applicants, licenses will be granted preferentially to applicants whose operations best promote the objectives of the Electronic Communication Services Act. Licenses may also be made available by way of an auction arrangement. According to the Electronic Communication Services Act, the licenses are not transferable other than within a group and even in case of an intra-group transfer, the Council of State must be notified immediately. If the effective control of the license-holder changes, the Council of State must be notified immediately and shall thereafter determine within two months whether the license will be annulled.

[262] In case a license application is not required, a written notification of the intention to operate public telecommunications must be submitted to Traficom before commencing operations. When the public telecommunications is temporary in nature, aimed at a small audience or otherwise of minor significance, notification is not needed.

Significant Market Power

[263] Within the context of the Electronic Communications Services Act, significant market power means that an operator is seen to exert such economic influence in a particular market, either alone or with others, that allows it to act independently of competitors, consumers or other users. Traficom conducts a market analysis of relevant markets to determine the competitive landscape from time to time. Such market analysis shall be completed no later than within two years of the European Commission issuing a market recommendation and at least every three years if the market has already been determined. Based on its market analysis,

Traficom may declare an electronic communications operator to be an operator with significant market power. There are particular obligations imposed on an operator with significant market power, which are set out in further detail in the Electronic Communications Services Act.

Television and Radio Operations and Other Communications

Television and Radio Operation

[264] In 2015, the Communications Market Act and the Act on Television and Radio Operations were repealed and replaced with the Information Society Code (917/2014), which entered into force on 1 January 2015 and was renamed as the Electronic Communications Services Act in 2018. Both television and radio operations are subject to licensing. Among other things, the Electronic Communications Services Act also regulates a television broadcaster's right to determine the programmes it will show. For example, pursuant to section 210 of the act, a television broadcaster shall reserve 19% of its broadcasting time for programmes produced by independent European producers or alternatively 19% of the broadcaster's programming budget. At least 50% of the programming produced by such independent producers must be produced during the five immediately preceding years. There are also specific regulations concerning, for example, advertising and programmes which may cause detriment to the development of children.

The Finnish Broadcasting Company (YLE)

[265] The operations of the Finnish broadcasting company, YLE, are regulated by the Act on the Finnish Broadcasting Company. YLE is responsible for the provision of comprehensive television and radio programming for all citizens under equal conditions. The operations of YLE were funded through television license fees until the end of 2012. Since the beginning of 2013, YLE's costs have been funded by a public service broadcasting tax, which is calculated based on taxpayers' taxable income. The company is not permitted to broadcast advertisements.

Postal Services

[266] The Finnish postal services are regulated under the Postal Act (415/2011, as amended). The purpose of the Postal Act is to ensure the availability of universal postal services on equal terms in Finland. Posti Oy has been appointed by Traficom to provide universal postal services in Finland.

Broadband Data Connections

[267] The objective of the Ministry of Transport and Communications is to ensure the availability of fast data connections and services for all households and businesses. Originally, the aim was that nearly all permanent residences, business offices and public-sector offices would be located within 2 km of an optic fibre network or a cable network that enables data connections with a transfer speed of 100 Mb/s by the end of 2015. However, the goal was not reached by 2015 due to implementation problems. The current objective of the Ministry of Transport and Communications is to support the establishment of fast broadband data connections in areas that are not commercially reachable. Governmental subsidies will be paid for such purpose until 2021 and the Ministry of Transport and Communications will start preparations for continuing governmental subsidies for broadband construction. The continuation of the aid scheme is included in the Government Programme, and the new aid programme was established in 2021.

3 ANTITRUST/COMPETITION/FOREIGN DIRECT INVESTMENT ISSUES

3.1 Antitrust Legislation and Competent Authorities

[268] The principal law concerning competition issues in Finland is the Competition Act (948/2011, as amended). The Competition Act covers issues relating to anti-competitive behaviour and cooperation between competitors as well as abuse of dominance. It also sets forth the provisions relating to merger control. Other relevant legislation relating to merger control include the Government Decree on the Calculation of Turnover of a Party to a Concentration (1011/2011, as amended) and the Government Decree on the Obligation to Notify a Concentration (1012/2011, as amended).

[269] The Finnish Competition and Consumer Authority (FCCA) is an independent regulatory and supervisory authority in the field of competition law. The FCCA operates under the Finnish Ministry of Employment and the Economy. The main task of the FCCA is to protect sound and effective economic competition. It also has the right to intervene, where necessary, in restrictive practices, such as cartels and abuse of dominant position, violating the Competition Act and Articles 101 and 102 of the Treaty on the Functioning of the European Union (TFEU), which form the basis of competition policy. Competition restrictions are investigated both on the FCCA's own initiative and on the basis of complaints received from third parties.

[270] Where necessary, the FCCA makes proposals to the Market Court proposing that the Market Court should impose penalty payments on those who violate the competition rules. The decision of the Market Court can be appealed to the Supreme Administrative Court, which is the highest judicial body resolving upon competition issues. The penalty payment may also be imposed on an undertaking or an association of undertakings to whom the business activity involved in the infringement has been transferred as a result of a concentration or other corporate transaction.

3.2 Merger Control

[271] Merger control provisions were first introduced in Finland in 1998. The EU merger control provisions have been applicable to Finnish mergers since 1995, when Finland became a Member State of the EU. Today, the Finnish merger control provisions are applied to transactions which meet the national thresholds. Transactions which fall within the scope of the EU merger control provisions, namely Council Regulation (EC) No. 139/2004 on the control of concentrations between undertakings (as amended), need to be notified to the European Commission.

[272] Concentrations exceeding certain turnover thresholds must be notified to the FCCA under the Competition Act and the transaction must not be implemented prior to the FCCA's decision in the matter. If the FCCA identifies in its assessment that the transaction may significantly impede effective competition in the relevant markets, the FCCA may impose structural conditions upon it, for example, an obligation to divest. Alternatively, the FCCA can impose conditions on the merged entity's future behaviour, such as licensing and supply obligations.

[273] The proposed merger may also be prohibited altogether, if a satisfactory conclusion cannot be obtained by imposing conditions. The acquisition may be prohibited by the Market Court upon the proposal of the FCCA. In 2019, the FCCA approved thirty-four merger decisions in total, four of which with conditions.

[274] In 2011, the FCCA issued Guidelines on Merger Control (1/2011, as amended). The objective of the Guidelines on Merger Control is to clarify the principles adhered to in the interpretation of the provisions on merger control and to provide more detailed instructions on the application of the provisions. The Guidelines on Merger Control deal with issues such as the notification obligation and procedure, the calculation of turnover and the assessment of mergers.

3.2.1 Scope of Application

[275] Pursuant to section 22 of the Competition Act, a concentration must be notified with the FCCA if the combined turnover of the parties to the concentration exceeds EUR350 m and the individual turnover of at least two of the parties, accumulated from Finland, exceeds EUR20 m. However, the turnover thresholds are expected to be amended, and the amendments to the Competition Act are in preparation.

[276] In the context of the Finnish merger control regulations, a concentration means: (i) the acquisition of control or an acquisition of a corresponding actual control (control); (ii) the acquisition of the entire business operations or a part thereof of an undertaking; (iii) a merger; or (iv) the creation of a joint venture which shall perform on a lasting basis all the functions of an autonomous economic unit. As in the EU law context, the provisions on the control of concentrations shall not apply to internal arrangements within a group of companies.

[277] Moreover, as stated above, the provisions of the Competition Act concerning the control of concentrations do not apply if the concentration falls within the scope of the above-mentioned Council Regulation on the control of concentrations between undertakings, unless the European Commission refers the concentration to the FCCA. The European Commission has the sole right to examine concentrations having a community dimension.

3.2.2 Assessment of Concentrations

[278] Under the Competition Act, the FCCA uses the so-called SIEC test in their assessment of concentrations. Pursuant to the SIEC test, the FCCA intervenes with a concentration if, as a result of it, the concentration may 'significantly impede effective competition' in the Finnish markets or a substantial part thereof, in particular as a result of the creation or strengthening of a dominant position. From the perspective of the appraisal process, the test is designed specifically to measure how much competition is lost as a result of the merger. The future development of the markets is also sought to be taken into consideration as well as the views of the main competitors to the parties to the concentration, customers and suppliers alike.

3.2.3 Notification Procedure and Timing

[279] The parties of the concentration may request a preliminary meeting with the FCCA to discuss beforehand the planned arrangement. Also, the parties may request advice in relation to the documents to be provided and some particular questions of the case which are of interest to the FCCA. Pursuant to the FCCA, such preliminary discussions are not mandatory but may facilitate drafting the notification and serve to help the FCCA to process the matter quickly.

[280] It is common that the parties to the transaction discuss the filing and may present their plans to the FCCA jointly. However, pursuant to the Competition Act, the acquiring party has an obligation to notify the transaction. If the transaction concerns a joint venture, the parties forming the joint venture have a joint obligation to notify the transaction.

[281] Under the Competition Act, there is no fixed deadline within which the concentration should be notified to the FCCA. Under the Competition Act and, in particular, pursuant to section 23, a concentration must be notified to the FCCA following the conclusion of the agreement, acquisition of control, or the announcement of a public bid but prior to the implementation of the transaction. A concentration may also be notified to the FCCA as soon as the parties demonstrate with sufficient certainty their intention to conclude a concentration. The notification must be completed in accordance with the detailed instructions set out in the Government Decree on the Obligation to Notify a Concentration (1012/2011). The decree also lists the information to be provided in the notification.

[282] After the notification has been submitted, the FCCA has 23 business days to decide either to clear the transaction or to open an in-depth investigation of the transaction (phase two). In case the FCCA does not decide to move the transaction into a phase two investigation, the transaction is considered to be approved. In phase two, the FCCA has a period of sixty-nine business days to investigate the case further. Within the three-month period, the FCCA must either approve the transaction, with or without conditions, or propose to the Market Court that the transaction be prohibited. The Market Court may decide upon request to grant an additional forty-six business days for the phase two investigation.

[283] The parties to the concentration cannot take measures to implement the concentration before the FCCA has given its final approval without conditions, or with conditions attached. In case of special circumstances, the parties to the concentration may request the FCCA to grant an exemption permission to implement the transaction prior to its final approval. In case of a tender offer (mandatory or voluntary) referred to in the Securities Market Act or the use of a redemption right or obligation referred to in the Companies Act, the prohibition to implement the transaction prior to FCCA's approval does not apply.

[284] In case the FCCA has made a proposal to the Market Court to prohibit a concentration, the Market Court must issue its decision on the case within three months from the FCCA's proposal. If no decision is received, the transaction is considered to be approved. The decision of the Market Court may be appealed to the Supreme Administrative Court, which is the highest appellate court in proceedings relating to competition law.

3.2.4 Sanctions

[285] As mentioned above, the parties to the concentration cannot implement or take any actions to implement the transaction prior to its approval by the competition authorities. Breach of the obligation not to implement the transaction prior to it being approved may result in penalty payments (fines) being imposed. Penalty payments will not be imposed if the conduct is deemed minor or the imposition of a penalty payment is otherwise unjustified with respect to safeguarding competition. The FCCA decides upon the penalty payment and its amount. The amount of the penalty payment will be based on an overall assessment by the FCCA and it may not exceed 10% of the turnover of the undertaking concerned.

3.3 Foreign Direct Investments

[286] Under certain situations where key national interests require restricting the transfer of influence to foreign investors in a corporate transaction, prior approval from the Ministry of Economic Affairs and Employment of Finland or other additional clearances may be required pursuant to the Act on Monitoring Foreign Acquisitions (172/2012, as amended). Furthermore, the Ministry serves as national contact point for the EU Regulation 2019/452 of the European Parliament and of the Council of 19 March 2019 establishing a framework for the screening of foreign direct investments into the Union.

[287] In practice, key national interests mainly consist of national defence and critical insecurity of supply materials as well as other functions that are considered fundamental to society. The Act on Monitoring Foreign Acquisitions defines a corporate transaction as activities as a result of which (i) a foreign owner gains control of at least one-tenth, (ii) at least one-third, or (iii) at least one-half of the aggregate number of votes conferred by all shares in the company, or a holding that otherwise corresponds to decision-making authority in a limited liability company or other monitored entity. Further, a foreign purchaser is defined as (i) a person who does not reside or company or corporation that does not have its domicile in the European Union or a country party to the European Free Trade Association; or (ii) a company or corporation that has its domicile within the EU or a Member State of the European Free Trade Association, but in which a person or entity referred to under (i) above holds at least one-tenth of the votes or corresponding de facto power.

[288] In respect of defence equipment industry, the monitoring covers all foreign investors. In the non-military sector, Finnish companies considered critical for securing vital functions of society are being monitored. It should, however, be noted that in respect of acquisitions within the defence sector, the restrictions also apply to such persons and entities that reside or are domiciled, as applicable, in the EU or a member of the European Free Trade Association (EFTA) other than Finland as well as Finnish entities where in other sectors, the monitoring only covers foreign investors residing or domiciled outside the EU or EFTA.

[289] The acquisitions in the defence and defence equipment industry as well as in the security sector always require prior confirmation by the authority (application). As regards the other corporate acquisitions, the foreign owner may also submit the acquisition for advance approval of the Ministry if the acquisition is in the phase immediately preceding the final implementation (notification). The Ministry may also require that the matter be submitted to the Ministry for examination in the formal confirmation process. The application and notification submitted to the Ministry of Economic Affairs and Employment is informal. However, the Ministry has published instructions for preparing the application/notification. Furthermore, the application and notification must also be accompanied by a form containing the information required by the EU Regulation. The application for a corporate acquisition under the Foreign Investment Control Act must contain all information on the target entity, the foreign party, and the corporate acquisition necessary for consideration of the clearance.

[290] After having received the necessary documentation, the Ministry requests statements from other authorities to the extent required. Furthermore, the Ministry considers if it is required to notify the other EU Member States and the Commission under the EU regulation. After having received the statements from the other authorities, the Ministry makes a decision: a confirmation on the corporate acquisition or it refers the matter for consideration in a government plenary session if the corporate acquisition has potential for conflict with a key national interest. There are no exact time limits for processing the application. There have been only very few applications each year and it appears that no transaction has been refused by the Council of State due to a potential conflict with a key national interest.

3.4 Real Estate Acquisitions by Foreign Entities

[291] As of 1 January 2020, subject to limited exceptions, real estate acquisitions by foreign entities and persons domiciled outside the EU and the EEA require permission from the Finnish Ministry of Defense. The restrictions also apply to transferees that have their registered office in the EU or EEA but in which a natural person or an entity residing outside of the EU and the EEA holds at least one-tenth of the total voting rights or equivalent influence over the transferee. Restricted entities may acquire real property in Finland only if the Ministry of Defense grants permission for such acquisition. The new legislation applies to properties located throughout Finland, with the exception of the Åland Islands. Permission for the acquisition must be obtained prior to the transfer of property or within two months from the completion of the transfer and can be granted if the acquisition is not expected to impede organizing national security, supervision and safeguarding of territorial integrity, the maintenance of border control, border security or the maintenance of emergency stocks of critical supplies. If no permission is granted, the transferee must transfer the property back to the transferor within one year from the date the decision has become final. As of 14 December 2021, the Ministry of Defense has not declined permissions for real estate acquisitions, the act being applicable for almost two years.

3.5 Foreign Exchange Control

[292] Shares in Finnish companies may be purchased by non-residents of Finland without any Finnish exchange controls. Non-residents may also receive dividends without any exchange controls, with the transfer of assets out of Finland being subject to payment by the company of withholding taxes in the absence of an applicable tax treaty. Non-residents having acquired shares in a Finnish limited liability company may receive shares pursuant to a bonus issue or through participation in a rights issue without any Finnish exchange controls. Shares in a Finnish company may be sold in Finland by non-residents, and the proceeds of such sale may be transferred out of Finland in any convertible currency. There are no Finnish exchange control regulations restricting the sale of shares in a Finnish company by non-residents to other non-residents.

4 TAXATION ASPECTS

4.1 Income Taxation

4.1.1 Income Taxation of Residents

[293] Finnish residents are subject to national and municipal income taxation in Finland for their worldwide income. Generally, an individual is deemed a Finnish resident if such individual stays in Finland for more than six consecutive months or if the permanent home and dwelling of such individual is in Finland. Earned income (e.g., salary) of resident individuals is taxed by the state at progressive rates and by municipalities (and optionally also by the church) at flat rates. Capital income is taxed at a flat rate by the state and the applicable tax rate is currently 30% or, to the extent that taxable capital income exceeds EUR30 000, 34%.

[294] Corporate entities registered under the laws of Finland and corporate entities registered under the laws of a jurisdiction other than Finland having a place of effective management in Finland are regarded as residents of Finland. The legal form of the corporate entity will largely determine its status in income taxation. Entities established as limited liability companies or cooperative societies are, independently from their owners, liable to pay corporate income tax on all of their worldwide income. The corporate income tax rate is currently 20%.

[295] In respect of self-employed professional individuals (*ammatinharjoittaja*), self-employed business entrepreneurs, general partnerships and limited partnerships, the profits of the business entity are fully taxable as the income of the owner entrepreneur(s). In such case, the taxable income attributable to the operation of the trade or business is, based on calculation principles set forth in the law, divided into a capital-income portion (taxed at the capital-income flat rate) and an earned-income portion (taxed at the earned-income progressive rate). The income of an agricultural enterprise is similarly divided into a capital-income portion and an earned-income portion. Further, certain associations or foundations promoting the public good (*yleishyödyllinen yhteisö*) are liable for income tax only for any receipt of business income or for any income derived from real property.

4.1.2 Income Taxation of Non-residents

[296] Non-residents of Finland are not generally liable for tax in Finland and are taxed only on certain types of income received from Finnish sources (e.g., dividends, rental income and capital gains related to holdings of Finnish real property and buildings). To the extent that a non-resident is deemed to have a permanent establishment in Finland, all income derived from such permanent establishment is generally taxable in Finland. Interest payments to non-residents are generally exempt from Finnish tax at source.

[297] Foreign taxes are credited against Finnish taxes only to the extent that they have been collected as provided by the relevant tax treaty. Removal of any international double taxation is requested on the income tax return.

4.1.3 Withholding Tax Relating to Dividends

[298] Non-residents of Finland are, as a general rule, subject to Finnish withholding tax on dividends paid by a Finnish company. The withholding tax is withheld by the company distributing the dividend at the time of dividend payment. Generally, the withholding tax rate is 20% for non-resident corporate entities and 30% for other non-residents. However, Finland has entered into double taxation treaties with many countries pursuant to which the applicable withholding tax rate is often reduced to 0%–15%. The benefit of such a reduced withholding tax rate is available if the person beneficially entitled to the dividend has provided to the payer of the dividend a valid tax card or necessary details of its nationality and identity. For nominee-registered shares, the current applicable tax-at-source rate has usually been 30%, as the dividend beneficiary is often unidentified at the time of payment. Dividends paid to nominee-registered shares held by a Finnish tax resident are subject to a 50% withholding tax if the information on the dividend beneficiary is not given. Further unidentified dividend beneficiaries will be subject to 35% tax at source and 30% tax-at-source rate will be applicable in cases where the beneficiary has been identified, but it is unclear at what rate the tax at source should be withheld. For example, the dividend beneficiary can be identified as an investment fund, but it is unclear whether the investment fund is entitled to treaty benefits. The 30% and 35% tax-at-source rates are being applied to dividends paid on 1 January 2021 or thereafter.

[299] No Finnish withholding tax is levied on dividends paid to foreign corporate entities that reside, and are subject to corporate tax, in an EU Member State as specified in Article 2 of the Council Directive 2011/96/EU of 30 November 2011 on the common system of taxation applicable in the case of parent companies and subsidiaries of different Member States and that directly hold at least 10% of the capital of the distributing Finnish company. Further, dividends paid to certain foreign corporate entities residing within the EEA are either fully tax-exempt or taxed at a reduced withholding tax rate depending upon how the dividend would be taxed if paid to a corresponding resident corporate entity. Also, under certain conditions, dividends paid to certain individuals residing within the EEA can be, upon request by such non-resident individual, taxed pursuant to the Act of Taxation Procedure (i.e., similarly as Finnish residents are taxed).

4.2 Value Added Tax

[300] The main indirect tax in Finland is value added tax (VAT) which is charged on imports and on sales of goods and services sold in Finland by businesses. The self-supply of goods and services by an entrepreneur is also considered as a taxable sale. A transfer of business does not constitute a taxable sale of goods and/or services provided that the buyer continues the business. Also minor sales (turnover for a twelve-month accounting period from 1 January 2021 onwards is at most EUR15 000) are exempt from VAT.

[301] As a general rule, the seller is liable for collecting the VAT (by adding it to the price) and remitting it to the state. As VAT is a consumption tax payable by the final consumer, the seller has the right to deduct any VAT included in his purchases of goods and services for business purposes (provided that a supplier liable for VAT has supplied them to him).

[302] The general VAT rate effective in respect of most goods and services is 24% from the beginning of 2013. The VAT rate is, however, lower for certain goods and services: 14% in respect of food and restaurant services, and 10% in respect of books, cultural events, transportation services and medicine. In addition, certain forms of business specified in Finnish tax law have been left outside the scope of VAT, including healthcare services, financial services (including the sale of shares), insurance services as well as sale of real property or apartments in housing companies. Renting of real property or apartments is also generally exempted from VAT, but it is, under certain conditions, possible to register for VAT in which case the rental income from the property will be subject to VAT, but also any VAT included in goods and services acquired in relation to the property can be deducted.

[303] VAT registration in Finland is mandatory for any business for which VAT is payable. Companies registered for VAT in Finland are liable to submit periodic tax returns to report all VAT information for each taxable period as well as remitting the amount of VAT payable to the tax authorities. The taxable period is usually one month (or, for certain minor businesses, a year or quarterly period).

4.3 Asset Transfer Tax

[304] Transfer of real property (i.e., real estate, parts thereof as well as certain buildings and certain land lease agreements) and Finnish securities (e.g., shares, certain bonds and certain subscription rights) are usually subject to transfer taxation.[1] In respect of real property, the transfer tax rate is 4%. In respect of securities, the transfer tax rate is currently 1.6% on all securities except for shares in housing and real estate companies and foreign securities, in respect of which the transfer tax rate is 2%. Transfer tax is payable on the purchase price or on the value of any other consideration used as the means of payment. Transfer tax is not payable in connection with the issuance or subscription of new shares (however, if such new shares are paid in kind by using real property or securities, the company issuing shares is liable for transfer tax).

[305] Usually, transfer tax is not payable on the transfer of shares that are publicly traded. This exemption requires, among other things, that a securities broker, as defined in the law, is brokering or acting as a party to the transaction, or that the transferee has been approved as a trading party in the market where the transfer is executed. Further, the transfer tax exemption does not apply to certain transfers (e.g., transfers executed as equity investments or distribution of funds).

[306] Except for transfers of shares in housing or real estate companies, no transfer tax is payable if neither party to the transaction is generally liable for tax in Finland or a Finnish branch or office of a foreign credit institution, investment service firm or fund management company. As a general rule, the buyer is liable for the

[1] As of 1 Mar. 2013, foreign securities have also been subject to transfer taxation when the business of such foreign company is to own or manage, directly or indirectly, real property and at least 50% of its total assets comprises of directly or indirectly owned real property located in Finland, provided that at least one party to the transfer is a Finnish tax resident or a Finnish branch or office of a foreign credit institution, investment service firm or fund management company.

tax, but the parties may agree otherwise. If only the buyer is not a Finnish tax resident, or a Finnish branch or office of a foreign credit institution, investment service firm or fund management company, the seller must collect the tax from the buyer.

4.4. Acquisition of Business

[307] A business may be acquired in various ways, the two most common being the acquisition of assets (asset transaction) and the acquisition of shares (share transaction). Prior to entering into the transaction, taxation aspects of both options should be analysed carefully.

4.4.1 Asset Transaction

[308] In respect of taxation, an asset transaction is usually beneficial to the buyer as the buyer may generally depreciate the whole acquisition price, usually with the exception of the portions of the purchase price allocated to land, securities and similar assets, which are not subject to wear and tear. As a general rule, the purchase price is allocated to the acquired assets on the basis of their fair market values. The seller incurs either taxable income or deductible loss depending upon whether or not the remaining acquisition costs of the assets in taxation exceeds the acquisition price. If the total acquisition price exceeds the aggregate fair market value of all acquired assets (minus assumed liabilities), the difference is allocated as goodwill for the buyer. Goodwill can be deducted in corporate taxation, usually over a period of maximum of ten years. If the acquired assets include real property or securities, transfer tax is payable for such assets (*see* the above paragraphs [304]–[306]).

4.4.2 Share Transaction

[309] In a share transaction, the acquisition price forms the acquisition cost of the shares and thus is non-deductible until the shares are sold or otherwise transferred or a substantial deterioration in value occurs. A share transaction entails more risks than an asset transaction as the buyer assumes the whole company with all of its assets and liabilities. Therefore, a thorough tax due diligence should always be conducted. Transfer tax is usually payable for the whole acquisition price of the shares (*see* the above paragraphs [304]–[306]). It should be noted that transfer tax is always payable on the whole acquisition price, including any possible earn-out or other conditional parts of the purchase price. In such a situation, the likely amount of earn-out to be payable to the seller must be determined. In case the earn-out is later determined to the effect that it differs from the amount estimated at the time of paying the transfer tax, the excess may be claimed back or supplemental transfer tax must be paid. If the amount of earn-out cannot be objectively determined, transfer tax may be payable after the final amount of earn-out has become evident. In a share transaction, the status of any confirmed losses of the target company should also always be taken into account (*see* below for paragraph [319]).

4.4.3 Mergers and Demergers

[310] Under Finnish corporate law, corporations can merge in various ways. However, for a merger to qualify as a tax-exempt transaction under Finnish tax law, one or more limited liability companies (a merging company) must, by dissolving without liquidation, transfers all of its assets and liabilities to another limited liability company (a receiving company) and the shareholders of the merging company receive as a merger consideration shares issued by the receiving company pro rata to their shareholding or at most 10% cash calculated from par value or paid in capital. In addition, a merger qualifies as a merger in taxation when the receiving company, or its fully owned subsidiary, holds all the shares in the merging company. Should a merger not fulfil these conditions, the merging company shall be deemed as dissolved in taxation. It should be noted that a triangular merger, where a third party other than the receiving company gives merger consideration, is permitted under Finnish corporate law but it does not qualify as a merger under Finnish tax legislation.

[311] In a merger under Finnish tax legislation, the acquisition costs of the merging company are deducted in the receiving company's taxation in the same manner as they would have been deducted in the merging company's taxation. For the year of the merger, the maximum depreciations of the receiving company are decreased by the amount of depreciations allowed in the merging company's taxation for such year. The profit incurred by the merger is not taxable nor the loss deductible. The acquisition cost of the shares received as merger consideration is the value equal to the acquisition cost of the shares in the merging company.

[312] The above also applies to a demerger. However, the acquisition cost of the shares in a receiving company is equal to the net value of the property transferred to the receiving company.

[313] The provisions regarding a merger and a demerger are also applicable in a situation where the receiving company is a company incorporated in another EU Member State, provided that the transferred assets de facto remain relating to the receiving company's place of business in Finland.

4.5 Deductibility of Acquisition Expenses

4.5.1 Asset Transaction

[314] Transaction costs relating to an asset transaction, including, *inter alia*, the costs of financial and legal advisors, can usually be deducted in taxation as business costs. However, any transfer tax paid in respect of real property or securities is considered as part of the respective acquisition cost.

4.5.2 Share Transaction

[315] Transaction costs relating to a share transaction generally may not be deducted directly as business expenses but will be included in the acquisition cost of the shares. Therefore, acquisition expenses in a share transaction only become deductible when the shares are sold or a substantial deterioration in value occurs.

4.6 Acquisition Financing Through Group Loans

[316] Interest on intra-group loans granted to Finnish companies for business purposes is generally fully deductible on an accrual basis, subject, however, to certain specific limitations on the deductibility of interest expenses described in further detail below. Further, such interest is, directly according to Finnish tax laws, exempted from Finnish withholding tax, provided that the loan cannot be deemed to constitute equity of the Finnish debtor.

[317] As a rule, Finnish tax laws do not include thin capitalization rules which would limit the possibility to deduct interest expenses. Currently, Finnish tax laws provide exemptions from certain limitations on interest deductibility as described further, provided that the company matches or exceeds certain intra-group metrics. However, if an intra-group loan were to include elements of equity, the Finnish tax authorities could deem the loan or a part thereof to be comparable to equity capital and accordingly, could limit the deductibility of interest expenses for tax purposes for such loans.

[318] As of 1 January 2019, the Finnish Government proposal concerning the implementation of the EU ATAD I-Directive (2016/1164) came into force, expanding the scope of interest deductibility restrictions as well as the definition of interest in taxation. The new limitations on interest deductibility apply if total net financing expenses (including both internal and external financing) exceed a threshold of EUR500 000, which is applied at the level of each individual company. To the extent that net financing expenses do not exceed EUR500 000 in a tax year, all financing expenses are deductible. Financing expenses include interest expenses on all forms of debt, other costs equivalent to interest as well as costs incurred in connection with raising financing. In the event that net financing expenses exceed EUR500 000, the limitations apply to the total net financing expenses, rather than just the amount exceeding the threshold and deductible net financing expenses are limited to 25% of the company's EBITD (i.e., taxable income including group contributions, added with interest expenses and tax depreciation). Notwithstanding the foregoing, external net financing expenses are always fully deductible up to a safe harbour of EUR3 000 000, provided that they exceed the aforementioned threshold of 25% of the company's EBITD and are to be deducted in advance of internal financing expenses. In addition to the safe harbour regarding external net financing expenses, there are also certain exceptions relating to financing expenses on third-party debt incurred prior to 17 June 2016, which may, under certain circumstances, be excluded from the scope of the limitations. In addition, among

other things, companies in the financial services sector (e.g., financial institutions, insurance companies) and interest expenses relating to certain public infrastructure projects may fall outside the scope of the limitations. Further, if the equity to assets ratio of the company is higher than the corresponding ratio on the consolidated group level and provides sufficient evidence thereof as specified in further detail in the relevant legislation, the interest deductibility limitations will not apply. It is also worth noting that receivables security granted as security for a third-party loan and certain back-to-back arrangements where a related party has a receivable from a third-party, which is related to the relevant third-party loan, are deemed to result in such third-party loan being considered a related party loan for the purposes of the interest deductibility limitations, meaning that the safe harbour mentioned above would not apply. In the event that the deductibility of interest is limited by the above rules, any financing expenses that are non-deducible can be carried forward in perpetuity.

4.7 Confirmed Losses

[319] The Finnish system of tax losses is based on carryforward principles meaning that confirmed losses may be carried forward to be deducted from the profits of future years. Losses incurred by corporate entities during the financial year may be carried forward for ten subsequent years. The corporate entity may, however, lose the ability to carryforward losses if more than 50% of the shares or stakes of the entity directly change ownership. Same also applies in case of an indirect change in ownership (i.e., a similar change in ownership in the entity owning at least 20% of the entity which has incurred the losses). In case of publicly listed corporate entities, these amounts are calculated from the non-listed shares or stakes. For special reasons, if it is necessary for the continuance of the business of the corporate entity, the Tax Administration may grant an exemption to carry the losses forward irrespective of an ownership change as set forth above. It should also be noted that ownership changes are calculated cumulatively and, therefore, any consecutive changes of ownership after the year when the losses have first incurred will be taken into account. In a merger and demerger, the receiving company does not have the right to deduct tax losses unless the receiving company and/or its shareholders have owned more than half of the shares in the (de)merging company from the beginning of the loss year, and tax authorities cannot grant any exception to this.

4.7.1 Transfer Pricing

[320] The arm's length principle is internationally recognized in transfer pricing. Intra-group transactions should be priced without deviations from the arm's length principle, i.e., the same conditions and amounts should be used that would be used in the case of transactions between independent, non-associated parties. It is also expressed in tax laws. If the Finnish tax authorities observe deviations from the arm's length principle, they may reassess the income tax of the company and make an income tax adjustment. Taxation will be carried out as if the arm's length principle has been followed. When transfer pricing involves incomes that are generated in two or several tax jurisdictions or countries, careful documentation may prevent international double taxation.

5 EMPLOYMENT CONSIDERATIONS

5.1 Regulatory Framework

5.1.1 Employment Contracts Act and Other Applicable Laws

[321] The Finnish labour market system is regulated by employment law and industry-specific collective bargaining agreements. Employment law sets out the mandatory minimum conditions for employment relationships in industry sectors that do not have collective bargaining agreements but also includes provisions that may be altered through collective agreements. Provisions more favourable to the employee may always be adopted.

[322] The Employment Contracts Act (55/2001, as amended) is the main statute applicable to employment relationships. The Employment Contracts Act applies to employment contracts entered into by an employee, or jointly by several employees as a team, agreeing personally to perform work for an employer under the employer's direction and supervision in return for pay or some other remuneration. The Employment Contracts Act sets out, among other things, general rules and regulations, employees' and employers' obligations, statutory benefits as well as lay-off and termination of employment.

[323] Other relevant laws are, *inter alia,* the Cooperation Act (1333/2021)as amended the 'Cooperation Act'), the Annual Holidays Act (162/2005, as amended), the Working Hours Act (872/2019, as amended), the Occupational Safety and Health Act (738/2002, as amended) and the Employees Pensions Act (395/2006, as amended).

5.1.2 Collective Bargaining Agreements

[324] Collective bargaining agreements are agreements between employer and employee associations. They are usually industry-wide and define the minimum rights and obligations of the employer and the employees during the agreement period, which is usually a fixed term of two years. Collective agreements largely determine the contents of an employment relationship, such as wages, benefits, holidays and working hours.

[325] If a certain collective bargaining agreement is considered to be national and representative in the sector in question, it may be confirmed by a special commission appointed by the Finnish Government to be generally binding. This means that they are generally applicable to employment relationships that concern the work the employee performs or nearest comparable work. The employer must observe at least the provisions of a generally binding collective agreement. Any term and condition of an employment contract that is in conflict with an equivalent term in the generally binding collective agreement is void and superseded by such equivalent term and condition.

[326] During the term of the collective bargaining agreement, industrial actions (strikes), the right to which is generally guaranteed by the Constitution, are prohibited. Striking is permitted after an agreement has ended, and if the strike is lawful, employees are protected against dismissal and claims for damages.

5.1.3 The Cooperation Act

[327] The Cooperation Act is applicable to companies which employ at least twenty people. It sets out provisions regarding the continuous cooperation dialogue between the employer and employees in matters relating to, among others, the financial situation of the company or organization workplace rules and practices, personnel structure and competence needs, wellbeing at work. Further, the Cooperation Act sets out provisions on the change negotiations which must be carried out in the event the employer is planning changes in its business operations which significantly affect the personnel or which lead to redundancies, lay-offs or shifting employees to part-time work. In addition to the Cooperation Act, the provisions in the collective bargaining agreements need to be taken into consideration in matters within the scope of the Cooperation Act.

5.2 Employment Contracts and Benefits

5.2.1 Employment Contracts

[328] The Employment Contracts Act and the applicable collective bargaining agreement set out the minimum terms for the employment contract between the employer and the employee. The employer and the employee may always agree on more favourable terms to the employee.

[329] Based on its right of direction and supervision, the employer may unilaterally decide on certain changes to the work and working conditions of the employee. Such changes, however, cannot amend the terms of the employment contract. Any amendment to the employment contract needs to be mutually agreed upon between the employer and the employee. If such mutual agreement cannot be reached, the amendment may only be implemented by terminating the employment contract, provided that the grounds for termination exist, and subsequently entering into a new employment contract with the employee.

[330] An employer and an employee may freely and without a particularly weighty reason agree on the minimum duration of the employment relationship agreement on the condition that the contract is reasonable. However, subject to the Employment Contracts Act, an employment contract concluded for longer than five years may, when five years have elapsed from the conclusion of the contract, only be terminated on the same grounds and using the same procedure as an employment contract concluded for an indefinite period. An employer and an employee can also agree on contractual penalties concerning the minimum duration obligation.

5.2.2 Management Contracts

[331] The members of the company's management, excluding the managing director, are considered to be employees of the company and thus be covered by the employment law. However, there are certain exceptions which concern the management. For example, the Working Hours Act is not applicable to work which must be considered management of an undertaking, corporation or foundation or an independent part thereof by virtue of the relevant duties and of the employee's position otherwise, or independent work directly comparable to such management. Further, it is customary that the management is excluded from the scope of applicability of collective bargaining agreements.

[332] Under Finnish law, a managing director is not considered an employee but a separate corporate organ (similar to the board of directors), and therefore neither any of the collective bargaining agreements nor the Finnish employment laws and regulations generally apply to the managing director, unless otherwise agreed.

5.2.3 Agreement of Non-competition or Non-solicitation

[333] According to the Employment Contracts Act, an agreement made at the beginning of, or during the employment relationship, may limit the employee's right to conclude an employment contract with a competing firm and also the employee's right to engage in competing operations on his or her own account (agreement of non-competition). However, an agreement of non-competition can be made only for a particularly weighty reason and must always be compensated.

[334] An agreement of non-competition may restrict the employee's right to conclude a new employment contract or to engage in the relevant business for a maximum of twelve months. Compensation for a non-competition agreement must be paid in an amount depending on the salary of the employee and on the agreed duration of non-competition agreement (the restraint period). If the restraint period is no longer than six months, then the employer must pay 40% of the employee's salary for the corresponding period. If the restraint period is longer than six months, then the employer must pay 60% of the salary for the entire restraint period. Instead of compensation for loss, the agreement may include a provision on contractual penalty, which shall not exceed the amount of pay received by the employee for the six months preceding the end of the employee's employment relationship. To the extent that the non-compete agreement goes beyond the allowed restrictions set out in the Employment Contracts Act, such agreement will be null and void.

[335] What is provided above on restricting the duration of an agreement of non-competition and the maximum contractual penalty does not apply to employees who, in view of their duties and status, are deemed to be engaged in the direction of the enterprise, corporate body or foundation or an independent part thereof or to have an independent status immediately comparable to such managerial duties. Therefore it is allowed to agree on considerably longer non-competitive obligations as well as greater contractual penalties with, for example, managing directors and special experts. However, these conditions have to be reasonable. An agreement of non-competition does not bind the employee or the managing director if the employment relationship has been terminated for a reason deriving from the employer.

[336] An employer and an employee can also agree on confidentiality or that the employee is not allowed to entice away from the employer any employee of the company for a certain period of time (agreement of non-solicitation). The agreement may include a provision on contractual penalty.

5.2.4 Pension Arrangements and Social Security

[337] In Finland, all employers are obliged to pay certain insurance and social security contributions. Persons working in the private sector are insured in accordance with the Employees Pensions Act irrespective of an employee's field of work, earnings or length of the contract. The employer is liable to subscribe for pension insurance for all his employees between 18 and 68 years of age. The employer and the employee both pay their share of the pension contribution.

[338] The employer can choose the pension insurance company in which it insures its employees. The employment pension contributions are formed in every pension company on similar grounds on the basis of the employee's salary.

[339] In addition to the above-described mandatory pension insurance, the employer may arrange additional pension insurance for its employees. It is relatively customary that additional pension arrangements are made for the managing director or other members of the management. In an acquisition, the additional pension insurance follows the employee as a part of such employee's employment contract.

[340] The employer is obliged to pay the following further mandatory contributions with respect to its employees: (i) social security contributions to be paid to the tax authorities, (ii) accident insurance premium, the amount of which varies according to the sector or industry, and (iii) unemployment insurance premium. Additionally, the employer is obliged to take a mandatory group life insurance for its employees.

[341] A Finnish employer has to insure a foreign employee working in Finland in the same way as Finnish employees. A foreign employer is usually also liable to arrange pension provision under the Employees Pensions Act for its employees who work in Finland. An exception to this rule concerns employees whom a foreign employer sends to work in Finland. The Employees Pensions Act does not concern employees whom the foreign employer sends to Finland on a short assignment which lasts for a maximum of two years.

5.3 Transfer of Employees in Business Transfer

5.3.1 Principle of Continuity

[342] Employees will automatically transfer to the new employer in connection with a business transfer. According to section 10 of Chapter 1 of the Employment Contracts Act, the employees related to the transferred business and the employment-related rights, obligations and benefits under the relevant employment relationships transfer to the new owner. This means that the employees will transfer as 'old employees' and the employment relationships continue without any interruption. The transferor and the transferee are jointly and severally liable for the employee's pay or other claims deriving from the employment relationship that have fallen due before the transfer. Unless the parties to the transfer agree otherwise, the transferor is liable to compensate such claims pertaining to the time before the transfer to the transferee. Further, pursuant to section 5 of Chapter 7 of the Employment Contracts Act, a transfer of business is not, as such, a legal and sufficient ground to terminate any employment relationship.

5.3.2 Cooperation Procedure

[343] The Cooperation Act provides that the old and new employers must inform the affected employees in connection with a business transfer. Subject to the Cooperation Act, personnel shall have the right to participate in decision-making in executive, supervisory or advisory bodies of the undertaking when they are handling matters of importance to the business operations, finances, and the personnel's position in the undertaking. There is thus no obligation to consult with employees about the transfer and employee consent is not required in order for the transfer to take place.

[344] Both the old and new employer must provide the representatives of affected employees with the following information: (i) the timing or the proposed timing of the transfer, (ii) the reasons for the transfer, (iii) the legal, economic and social consequences of the transfer to the employees, and (iv) measures which are proposed that would affect the employees.

[345] The above-mentioned information must be given to the representatives of the affected employees by the old employer a sufficient time before the transfer takes place. There is no set timeframe for this, but case law has indicated that one or several weeks in advance of the transfer would suffice, depending on the time period between the decision on the transfer and the actual transfer taking place.

[346] The new employer must give such information to the representatives of the affected employees within one week after the transfer. In addition, the new employer must give the employee representatives an opportunity to ask further questions and answer such questions. Failure to inform employees of the transfer could result in a penalty payment.

6 ACCOUNTING TREATMENT IN FINLAND

[347] Finnish publicly listed companies must prepare their group accounts, with regard to the format and content, in accordance with IFRS as adopted by the EU together with International Accounting Standards (IAS) and may also apply IFRS in their company-level financial statements. Use of IFRS is also permitted for unlisted domestic companies in both consolidated and separate company statements. If a company does not apply IFRS, its accounting is to be prepared in accordance with the Finnish Accounting Act (1136/1997, as amended) and instructions and opinions published by the Accounting Board, which operates under the supervision of the Ministry of Economic Affairs and Employment of Finland. It is worth noting that the Accounting Board, from time to time, seeks guidance from IFRS when issuing opinions and recommendations, particularly in terms of matters that are not specifically dealt with in the Accounting Act.

6.1 Accounting Treatment for Business Combinations

[348] Companies may neither adopt different merger and acquisition accounting nor adopt various accounting treatments – a general principle under the Accounting Act is that the principles and methods applied in the preparation of financial statements must be applied consistently from one financial year to the next. If the Accounting Act is applied, acquisitions are treated in accordance with the acquisition method (Fi: *hankintamenomenetelmä*) which also includes costs directly related to the acquisition (e.g., legal fees and the fees of other professional advisors). Other costs related to an acquisition are to be recorded as costs for the relevant financial period. Potential deferred purchase price payments may be valued at fair value and should be assessed already at the time of making the acquisition and recorded as part of the acquisition cost. There is no generally applicable method for determining the valuation of the assets allocated to a receiving company in a merger, and the accounting treatment of mergers is typically largely based on recommendations of the Accounting Board and accounting practice unless IFRS applies as described below. Nevertheless, provisions of the Accounting Act regarding the preparation of group accounts and, in particular, the acquisition method (Fi: *hankintamenomentelmä*) are typically used as a starting point in merger accounting.

If IFRS is otherwise applied by an acquiring company, IFRS must also be applied for business combination. Under IFRS, business combinations are treated in accordance with the amended IFRS 3 – 'Business Combinations', which applies the acquisition method (*hankintamenomenetelmä*) to business combinations and the amended IAS 27 – 'Consolidated and Separate Financial Statements'. Under IFRS, all combinations are acquisitions, contingent purchase price is valued at fair value and any subsequent changes in it will be to the statement of income, rather than by adjusting goodwill. Additionally, expenses relating to the acquisition are not capitalized but recognized directly in the statement of income as an expense (e.g., for legal and other services rendered).

6.2 Accounting Treatment of Goodwill

[349] Under IFRS, in accordance with the acquisition method, the amount of goodwill arising from the combination is recognized and may not be amortized. Instead of being amortized, goodwill is tested for impairment on a yearly basis (or more often if there is a triggering event). Additionally, impairment charges may not be reversed and negative goodwill is recognized immediately in accordance with IFRS (the amended IAS 36 – 'Impairment of Assets'). The test for impairment is performed in connection with test of the 'Cash Generating Unit' by applying the bottom-up/top-down method where the book value of goodwill is allocated to the cash flow producing unit. Under the Accounting Act and the acquisition method set out therein, the acquisition cost of goodwill is generally capitalized and amortized over its useful life according to a predetermined plan. If the reporting entity is unable to estimate the useful life in a reliable manner, goodwill must be amortized for a maximum of ten years. In accordance with the acquisition method under the Accounting Act, negative goodwill may be recognized as a separate liability item in the balance sheet provided that a corresponding expenditure or loss is expected in the relevant subsidiary. Negative goodwill shall be recognized as income in the profit and loss accounts at the time when the corresponding expenditure or losses are recognized as an expense in the subsidiary's profit and loss accounts or when it is matched by realized income.

6.3 Accounting Treatment of Intangible Assets

[350] IFRS standards derive the definition of intangible assets (*aineettomat hyödykkeet*) from the IAS standards (the amended IAS 38 – 'Intangible Assets'). IAS 38 requires an entity to recognize an intangible asset if, and only if, it is identifiable and specific criteria are met. An identifiable intangible asset is separable and arises from contractual or other legal rights. The intangible asset must additionally be controllable by the acquirer and the asset must provide an expected financial gain. IAS 38 further specifies how to measure the carrying amount of intangible assets and requires specified disclosures regarding intangible assets. In addition to IAS 38, IFRS 3 also includes a list of intangible assets that satisfy the criteria of being recognized apart from goodwill, e.g., brands and licenses. Intangible assets having an indefinite useful life are recognized separately from goodwill and may not be amortized. Pursuant to the Accounting Act, the cost of intangible assets acquired against consideration, such as concessions, patents, licenses, trademarks and similar rights and assets, must be capitalized if these are estimated to generate income over a period spanning several financial years. Such capitalized acquisition cost must be amortized during its useful life according to a predetermined plan.

www.ingramcontent.com/pod-product-compliance
Ingram Content Group UK Ltd.
Pitfield, Milton Keynes, MK11 3LW, UK
UKHW020151290926
15471UKWH00004B/812

9 789403 524061